COMPLETE HEALTHY RENAL DIET COOKBOOK FOR BEGINNERS

A Simple Guide With Over 100 recipes of Tasty, Delicious And Nutritious Meals of Low Sodium, Potassium And Phosphorus To Help Manage Chronic Kidney Disease

BONUS: 14- Day Meal Plan

Gwendolyn J. Hall

Your kidneys are worth the investment of a healthy diet - and you're worth it too!

This book is a work of nonfiction. Any similarity to real persons, living or dead, is coincidental and not intended by the author.

Disclaimer

The information provided in this book is for general informational and educational purposes only. The author, Gwendolyn J. Hall, and the publisher make no representations or warranties of any kind, express or implied, about the completeness, accuracy, reliability, suitability, or availability of the information contained herein. Any reliance you place on such information is strictly at your own risk.

The book is not intended as a substitute for professional advice or medical, legal, or financial guidance. Readers are encouraged to seek advice, as necessary, from qualified professionals in their respective fields to address specific concerns or questions.

The author and publisher disclaim any liability for any loss or damage arising from the use of this book or its content. The author is not responsible for the content of external websites or resources linked within this book.

Every effort has been made to ensure that the information provided is accurate and up to date at the time of publication. However, the author and publisher do not guarantee or warrant that the information is free of errors or omissions. Changes in knowledge, laws, regulations, and circumstances may have occurred since the book's publication.

The views and opinions expressed in this book are solely those of the author and do not necessarily reflect the views or opinions of the publisher.

The author appreciates your understanding of the limitations of this book and encourages readers to use their own judgment and consult relevant experts when making important decisions based on the information provided herein.

A healthy kidney diet is a recipe for a happy, healthy life - enjoy it to the fullest!

About the Author

Gwendolyn J. Hall is a passionate writer and culinary enthusiast whose love for food and storytelling has brought her on a journey of culinary exploration and creativity. With a keen eye for detail and an insatiable curiosity for the world of flavors, Gwendolyn has dedicated herself to crafting both delectable dishes and captivating narratives.

Born and raised in a culturally diverse community, Gwendolyn developed a deep appreciation for the rich tapestry of global cuisines from an early age. This fascination with food's power to connect people and cultures became the driving force behind her culinary adventures.

Gwendolyn's writing reflects her commitment to making the art of cooking accessible to all, regardless of their culinary expertise. Her warm and engaging prose invites readers into the kitchen, encouraging them to embrace the joy of cooking, explore new flavors, and create memorable dining experiences.

With a background in nutrition and a penchant for creating recipes that are as nutritious as they are delicious, Gwendolyn has a special interest in health-conscious cooking. Her work often combines the pleasures of indulgent flavors with the principles of a balanced diet.

When she's not experimenting with new recipes or penning culinary tales, Gwendolyn can be found exploring local markets, attending cooking classes, or sharing her culinary insights with her community. Her writing and culinary creations have been featured in various publications, and she continues to inspire and delight readers with her passion for all things food-related.

Gwendolyn's dedication to the culinary arts, her zest for life, and her commitment to sharing the joys of cooking make her a respected voice in the world of food and writing. Through her work, she hopes to inspire others to embark on their own culinary journeys and discover the magic of flavors and storytelling that can be found in every meal.

A Renal diet is the gift that keeps on giving - to your kidneys, and to you!

TABLE OF CONTENTS

INTRODUCTION

In the quiet town of NutriVille, there was a renowned chef named Kathryn. She possessed a unique talent for crafting meals that were not only delicious but also supportive of kidney health. Her kitchen was a place where the art of cooking met the science of nutrition.

One day, a man named Tom came to Kathryn seeking guidance. He had been grappling with kidney issues and was daunted by the idea of a renal diet. Kathryn welcomed him warmly and explained that a renal diet was all about finding balance.

With kindness and expertise, Kathryn showed Tom how to create flavorful dishes while keeping a close watch on sodium, potassium, and phosphorus levels. Together, they explored fresh ingredients and discovered the magic of herbs and spices.

As days turned into weeks, Tom not only learned the principles of a renal diet but also became an adept cook in his own right. His health began to improve, and his outlook brightened.

In NutriVille, the story of the renal diet was a tale of healing through the culinary arts. Thanks to Kathryn's guidance, Tom had not only regained his health but also become a culinary enthusiast, sharing the gift of a renal diet with others in need. It was a story of hope, nourishment, and the power of a well-balanced meal.

Introduction to Renal Diet

A renal diet, also known as a kidney-friendly diet, is a specialized eating plan designed to promote kidney health and manage various kidney-related conditions such as chronic kidney disease (**CKD**) and kidney failure.

This diet focuses on maintaining optimal levels of important nutrients while minimizing the intake of substances that can stress the kidneys.

By following a renal diet, individuals can help alleviate strain on their kidneys, prevent further deterioration of kidney function, and manage associated health complications.

In the tapestry of human health, the kidneys are both artists and curators.

They sculpt the delicate balance of our internal environment, ensuring that life flows smoothly through the canvas of our bodies.

However, when the strokes of health encounter disruptions such as chronic kidney disease (**CKD**), the need for a new palette of nourishment arises—a palette known as the renal diet.

Imagine the renal diet as a gallery of choices, each frame housing a nutritional masterpiece that contributes to the intricate mosaic of kidney well-being.

This dietary approach isn't a restriction but rather an invitation to define our culinary narrative. It's a journey of wild ingredients not just for taste but also for restoration and harmony.

At its essence, the renal diet is a compass guiding us through the intricate terrain of nutrients.

It beckons us to understand the nuances of proteins, sodium, potassium, and phosphorus, the pigments that can either embellish or blur the canvas of our kidney function.

With each meal, we become painters, using the brushstrokes of ingredients to create a portrait of health.

Nutritional Principles of the Renal Diet:

The nutritional principles of a renal diet revolve around balancing key nutrients while limiting certain components to ensure kidney health. This diet emphasizes controlled intake of protein, sodium, potassium, and phosphorus, which are critical for kidney function.

Recommended Foods for a Renal Diet:

High-Quality Proteins: Lean sources of protein such as poultry, fish, eggs, and plant-based options like tofu and legumes are recommended.

Low-Potassium Fruits and Vegetables: Apples, berries, carrots, cabbage, and green beans are good choices, as they are lower in potassium.

Low-Phosphorus Foods: White bread, rice, and pasta, as well as eggs, are lower in phosphorus content.

Include sources of healthy fats such as nuts, avocados, and olive oil in your diet.

Limited Dairy: Choose low-phosphorus dairy or dairy alternatives in moderation.

Foods on a Renal Diet should be limited or avoided:

High-Potassium Foods: Bananas, oranges, tomatoes, spinach, and potatoes should be limited due to their higher potassium content.

High-Phosphorus Foods: Dairy products, processed foods, colas, and certain beans should be limited to manage phosphorus intake.

Processed and Packaged Foods: These often contain hidden sodium, phosphorus, and potassium, which can strain the kidneys.

Meal Planning For A Renal Diet

When planning meals for a renal diet, it's important to consider portion sizes and nutrient content.

Consulting a registered dietitian with expertise in renal nutrition can be incredibly helpful in creating personalized meal plans that meet individual needs while adhering to renal diet guidelines.

Strategies to Reduce Sodium Content

Fresh Ingredients: Opt for fresh, whole foods instead of processed items to naturally reduce your sodium intake.

Herbs and Spices: Enhance flavor with herbs, spices, and lemon juice instead of salt.

Limit Condiments: Use condiments and sauces sparingly, as they often contain high levels of sodium.

Rinse Canned foods: If using canned vegetables or beans, rinse them under water to reduce sodium.

Managing Potassium Intake:

Portion Control: Pay attention to the portion sizes of high-potassium foods.

Cooking Methods: Boiling vegetables in water and draining them can help reduce their potassium content.

Soaking: Soak high-potassium vegetables in water for a few hours before cooking to reduce potassium levels.

Controlling Fluid Intake:

Fluid intake is often restricted in kidney-related conditions to prevent fluid buildup. The amount varies based on individual factors, and it's essential to follow healthcare provider recommendations closely.

Monitoring fluid intake through measuring and tracking can be helpful.

In managing a renal diet, personalized guidance from a healthcare provider or registered dietitian is invaluable. The renal diet is tailored to the individual's specific needs, stages of kidney disease, and other medical conditions.

Adhering to the principles of this diet can significantly contribute to the maintenance of kidney health and overall well-being.

Who is at risk of developing CKD?

Chronic Kidney Disease (**CKD**) can affect a wide range of individuals, but certain factors can increase the risk of its development.

These risk factors include:

- **Diabetes**: Individuals with diabetes, especially if it is poorly controlled, are at a higher risk of developing CKD.
- Diabetes can damage the blood vessels and filtering units (nephrons) in the kidneys, leading to kidney damage over time.
- **High Blood Pressure (Hypertension)**: Hypertension is a leading cause of CKD. Elevated blood pressure can strain the blood vessels in the kidneys, impairing their ability to filter waste and fluid effectively.
- **Family History**: A family history of kidney disease can increase the risk of CKD. Genetic factors can play a role in kidney health.
- **Age**: The risk of CKD increases with age, especially after the age of 60. Kidney function naturally declines as people get older.
- **Cardiovascular Disease**: Conditions like heart disease and stroke can affect kidney function due to reduced blood flow to the kidneys.
- **Obesity**: Being overweight or obese can contribute to the development of various Health conditions, including diabetes and hypertension, which increase the risk of CKD.

- Smoking damages blood vessels and decreases blood flow to the kidneys, increasing the risk of kidney damage.

- **High Cholesterol:** High cholesterol levels can lead to atherosclerosis (narrowing of blood vessels), which can affect kidney function.

- **Autoimmune Diseases:** Conditions like lupus and other autoimmune disorders can cause inflammation in the kidneys, leading to kidney damage.

- **Urinary Tract Infections**: Frequent or untreated urinary tract infections can potentially lead to kidney infections and kidney damage.

- **Kidney Stones**: Repeated occurrences of kidney stones can harm the kidneys and increase the risk of CKD.

- **Exposure to Nephrotoxic Substances**: Long-term exposure to certain medications, chemicals, and toxins can damage the kidneys.

It's important to note that while these factors increase the risk of CKD, anyone can be at risk, even without any of these factors. Regular check-ups, maintaining a healthy lifestyle, managing chronic conditions, and staying hydrated are all important steps in preventing or managing CKD.

If you believe you might be at risk, discussing your concerns with a healthcare provider can help determine appropriate measures to safeguard your kidney health.

FAQ(s) about Renal Diet

Certainly, here are some frequently asked questions (**FAQs**) about the renal diet:

1. **What is a renal diet?**

A renal diet is a specialized eating plan designed to promote kidney health and manage kidney-related conditions such as chronic kidney disease (**CKD**) or kidney failure. It focuses on controlling intake of certain nutrients like protein, sodium, potassium, and phosphorus to support optimal kidney function.

2. **Who needs to follow a renal diet?**

Individuals with kidney conditions like **CKD,** kidney failure, or those at risk of kidney problems due to factors like diabetes, high blood pressure, or family history, may need to follow a renal diet. Consulting a healthcare provider or dietitian is essential to determine if a renal diet is appropriate.

3. What are the goals of a renal diet?

The primary goals of a renal diet are to manage kidney function, prevent further damage, and minimize complications associated with kidney conditions. This includes maintaining proper levels of key nutrients while reducing the intake of substances that can stress the kidneys.

4. What nutrients are typically restricted in a renal diet?

A renal diet usually involves monitoring and controlling protein, sodium, potassium, and phosphorus intake. These nutrients can have an impact on kidney function and fluid balance in the body.

5. Can I still enjoy flavorful meals on a renal diet?

Absolutely! While some ingredients might be limited, there are many ways to enhance flavor using herbs, spices, lemon juice, and other kidney-friendly seasonings.
Creative cooking techniques can result in delicious and satisfying meals that adhere to renal diet guidelines.

6. Is there a one-size-fits-all renal diet?

No, renal diets are often tailored to an individual's specific needs. The diet may vary based on the stages of kidney disease, lab results, and other medical conditions.
Consulting a registered dietitian with expertise in renal nutrition is crucial for creating a personalized and effective renal diet plan.

7. Can I eat out while following a renal diet?

Yes, eating out is possible with some planning. Look for restaurants with healthier options and be prepared to ask about ingredients, preparation methods, and substitutions.
Many restaurants are willing to accommodate dietary restrictions if you communicate your needs.

8. **Are there any beverages I should limit on a renal diet?**

Fluid intake may be restricted, especially in advanced stages of kidney disease. Beverages high in sodium, potassium, and phosphorus, like colas and certain fruit juices, should be limited. Water, herbal teas, and small amounts of clear juices may be better choices.

9. **Can I still have snacks on a renal diet?**

Yes, you can enjoy snacks within the guidelines of your renal diet. Opt for kidney-friendly snacks like unsalted nuts, rice cakes, low-potassium fruits, and vegetables. Be mindful of portion sizes and choose snacks that align with your dietary restrictions.

10. **Is it possible to manage kidney health solely through diet?**

Diet plays a significant role in managing kidney health, but it's often just one part of a comprehensive approach. Medications, regular medical check-ups, and lifestyle modifications are also essential components of managing kidney conditions effectively.

Remember, individual dietary needs can vary greatly, so consulting a healthcare provider or registered dietitian who specializes in renal nutrition is crucial before making any significant changes to your diet.

Are Vegan-plant based recipes ideal for a renal diet patient?

Vegan and plant-based diets can be suitable for individuals with kidney issues like chronic kidney disease (**CKD**), but they require careful planning. Here are some considerations:

Benefits of Vegan-Plant Based Diets for Renal Patients:

- Reduced Protein Intake: Plant-based diets are naturally lower in protein, which can be beneficial for people with CKD, especially in the later stages. A high protein diet may place additional stress on the kidneys.

- Lower Phosphorus and Potassium: Many plant-based foods are lower in phosphorus and potassium, two minerals that need to be monitored in a renal diet.

- Healthy Nutrients: Plant-based diets can be rich in antioxidants, fiber, and a variety of vitamins and minerals, which can support overall health.

Considerations:

- Protein Quality: For vegans, it's essential to focus on high-quality plant-based proteins like beans, lentils, tofu, and quinoa. However, protein intake should be monitored and adjusted to individual needs.

- Phosphorus and Potassium: While plant-based foods tend to be lower in these minerals, some, like certain legumes and nuts, can be relatively high. Careful selection and portion control are necessary.

- Sodium Intake: Some processed vegan products may be high in sodium. Renal patients should limit sodium to manage blood pressure and fluid balance.

- Adequate Calories: Renal patients may have increased energy needs, and plant-based diets can sometimes be lower in calories. Ensure adequate calorie intake.

- Consult a Dietitian: A registered dietitian, preferably one with experience in renal nutrition, can help tailor a vegan-plant based diet to meet individual needs, monitor nutrient levels, and avoid deficiencies.

It's important for individuals with kidney issues to work closely with healthcare professionals to create a dietary plan that is suitable for their specific stage of CKD and overall health. A plant-based diet can be a viable option, but it must be adapted to address the unique dietary requirements of renal patients.

Symptoms of CKD

Chronic Kidney Disease (CKD) is often referred to as a "*silent*" disease because its symptoms may not become noticeable until the later stages. However, as **CKD** progresses, the following symptoms and complications may arise:

- Fatigue: Feeling unusually tired and lacking energy, even after getting enough rest, is a common early symptom.

- Fluid Retention: Swelling, particularly in the legs, ankles, feet, and face, can occur due to the kidneys' reduced ability to eliminate excess fluid from the body.

- Changes in Urination: This can include increased frequency, especially at night (nocturia), decreased urine output, or foamy or bubbly urine.

- Blood in Urine: This may be a sign of damage to the kidneys' filtering units (nephrons) and requires medical attention.

- Puffy Eyes: Swelling around the eyes, especially in the morning, can be an early sign of fluid retention and kidney dysfunction.

- High Blood Pressure: Chronic kidney disease can lead to elevated blood pressure, or it can be a contributing factor.

- Loss of Appetite: A decreased desire to eat and changes in taste can result from the buildup of waste products in the blood.

- Nausea and Vomiting: The accumulation of waste products and electrolyte imbalance can lead to nausea and vomiting.

- Breathing Difficulties: Fluid accumulation in the lungs can cause breathing difficulties or shortness of breath.

- Muscle Cramps: Electrolyte imbalances, such as low calcium or potassium levels, can lead to muscle cramps and twitching.

- Itching (Pruritus): The accumulation of waste products in the blood can cause itching, often severe and generalized.

- Bone Health Issues: Kidney disease can affect the balance of minerals in the body, leading to weekend bones and an increased risk of fractures.

- Anemia: Decreased kidney function can lead to reduced production of red blood cells, resulting in anemia and fatigue.

It's important to remember that these symptoms can be caused by various other conditions as well. If you're experiencing any of these symptoms, especially if you have risk factors for **CKD**, it's crucial to consult a healthcare professional for proper diagnosis and treatment. Early diagnosis and treatment of **CKD** can reduce its development and enhance general kidney function.

Brief Explanation on the Stages of CKD

Chronic Kidney Disease (CKD) is typically categorized into five stages, each reflecting the level of kidney damage and decline in kidney function. These stages are determined based on the glomerular filtration rate (GFR), which is a measure of how well the kidneys are filtering waste and excess fluid from the blood.

Here's a brief explanation of each stage:

1. **Stage 1 (G1-G2): Kidney Damage with Normal or High GFR**
   - In this early stage, there is evidence of kidney damage, such as abnormal blood or urine test results, but the GFR is still within normal range (above 90 mL/min).
   - Kidney function is generally preserved, and individuals may not experience noticeable symptoms.

2. **Stage 2 (G3a-G3b): Mildly Decreased GFR**
   - Kidney damage is present, and the GFR begins to decline mildly (60-89 mL/min).
   - Like in Stage 1, individuals may not show symptoms at this stage, but healthcare monitoring is important to prevent further progression.

3. **Stage 3 (G3a-G3b): Moderately Decreased GFR**
   - Kidney function is moderately reduced (30-59 mL/min), and symptoms may start to become noticeable.
   - Common symptoms include fatigue, fluid retention, changes in urine output, and signs of anemia.

4. **Stage 4 (G4): Severely Decreased GFR**
   - Kidney function is significantly decreased (15-29 mL/min), and symptoms become more pronounced.
   - Fatigue, swelling, increased blood pressure, and other complications can arise. Anemia and bone health issues are common.

5. **Stage 5 (G5): Kidney Failure (End-Stage Renal Disease)**
   - Kidney function is critically low (less than 15 mL/min), and the kidneys are no longer able to adequately filter waste and fluid from the blood.
   - Individuals in Stage 5 **CKD** require dialysis or kidney transplantation to replace kidney function.
   - Symptoms are severe, including fatigue, fluid overload, electrolyte imbalances, and increased risk of complications.

It's important to note that the progression of **CKD** can vary widely among individuals, and early detection and management are key to slowing down its progression. Regular monitoring by healthcare professionals, lifestyle modifications, and adhering to prescribed treatments can help individuals manage their condition and maintain better kidney health.

How to Use This Renal Diet Book

Welcome to the culinary adventure that awaits within these pages! This book is not just a collection of recipes; it's your guide to exploring the world of flavors, embracing the joys of cooking, and creating delicious meals that will delight your senses. To make the most of your journey with this book, here's how to use it effectively:

1. **Explore the Table of Contents**: Begin by flipping through the table of contents. This will give you an overview of the recipes and help you plan your culinary journey. Whether you're looking for breakfast, lunch, or dinner ideas, you'll find them categorized for easy reference.

2. **Consider Your Dietary Preferences**: Keep in mind your dietary preferences and any dietary restrictions you may have. Many of the recipes in this book can be customized to suit different needs. Whether you're vegetarian, vegan, gluten-free, or have specific health goals, there are options for you.

3. **Plan Your Meals:** Use this book to plan your meals for the week or month. There's a diverse range of recipes available, so you can create meal plans that suit your taste and nutritional needs. Consider your schedule and cooking abilities when planning.

4. **Get Inspired**: These recipes are more than just instructions; they're an invitation to get creative in the kitchen. Feel free to experiment with ingredients, flavors, and cooking techniques. Add your personal touch to make each dish uniquely yours.

5. **Make a Shopping List:** Before you start cooking, review the ingredients for your chosen recipes and make a shopping list. By doing this, you can stay organized and guarantee that you have everything you need.

6. **Follow the Instructions**: Each recipe includes clear and easy-to-follow instructions. Read through the recipe before you begin cooking to familiarize yourself with the steps and cooking times.

7. **Enjoy the Process**: Cooking can be a joyful and meditative experience. Savor the sights, sounds, and scents of your kitchen as you prepare your meal. Cooking is not just about the destination; it's about the journey.

8. **Share Your Creations:** Food has a magical way of bringing people together. Bring your culinary delights to the attention of your loved ones. Invite them to join you on your culinary journey, or surprise them with a homemade meal.

9. **Keep Notes**: As you cook, consider keeping a journal of your experiences. Not any modifications you made to the recipes, what worked well, and what you'd do differently next time. This will help you refine your culinary skills.

10. **Embrace the Learning Curve**: Don't be discouraged by the occasional mishap in the kitchen. Mistakes are part of the learning process, and they often lead to culinary discoveries. Keep experimenting and improving your skills.

11. **Connect with the Author**: If you have questions, feedback, or simply want to share your culinary adventures, don't hesitate to connect with the author. You can often find them on social media or through their website.

Above all, remember that cooking is an art, and every meal you create is a masterpiece. Enjoy the journey of discovery, and may your culinary adventures be filled with delicious moments and delightful surprises.

Happy cooking!!!

BREAKFAST RECIPES

Blueberry Muffins

Chocolate Banana Oatmeal

Egg Salad Avocado Toast

Maple-Nut Granola

Maple Granola

Salsa Scrambled Eggs

Apple Oatmeal

Old-Fashioned Oatmeal

Southwest Baked Egg Breakfast Cups

Dried Cranberry Fruit Bars

Blueberry Muffins

Nutrition Facts (Per serving) Calories 275 Fat 9g Sodium 210g Carbs 44g Protein 5g Potassium 121 mg Phosphorus 100g

Prep time: 15 minutes Total time: 45 minutes Serving Size 12 muffins (1 serving = 1 muffin)

The aroma of freshly cooked blueberry muffins filling your home at breakfast time is perhaps the best taking pleasure in each tasty mouthful.

INGREDIENTS

½ cup salted butter •¼ cup of sugar •2 eggs •2 cups of milk(1%) •2 cups of general-purpose flour •2 tablespoons of Baking powder •½ teaspoon of Salt •2 ½ Fresh blueberries •(For topping) 2 tablespoons of sugar

DIRECTIONS

- Margarine and sugar should be combined with a mixer on low speed until frothy and creamy.
- One at a time, add eggs and combine after each addition.
- Sift the dry ingredients, then pour in the milk in intervals.
- Mix in by hand after mashing ½ cup of blueberries.
- Then manually mix in the remaining blueberries.
- Spray some vegetable oil over the pan's surface and the muffin tins. Place the muffin cups in the pan.
- Fill each muffin cup to the brim with the batter. Sprinkle sugar on tops of muffins.
- Bake for 25–30 minutes at 375 °F.
- Allow to cool in the pan for at least 30 minutes before gently

Chocolate Banana Oatmeal

Nutrition Facts (Per serving) Calories 295 Fat 8.7g Sodium 281g Carbs 50g Protein 6.6g Potassium 408 mg Phosphorus 189g

Prep time: 10 minutes Total time: 10 minutes Serving Size 1 serving

With this kid-friendly healthy chocolate and banana oatmeal dish, you can enjoy your fruit and a little luxury, too. In a rush in the morning? Try this oatmeal variant overnight.

INGREDIENTS

1 cup of water •A dash of salt •½ cup rolled old-fashioned oats •½ sliced tiny banana •1 tablespoon of chocolate-hazelnut spread •A pinch of salty seaweed

DIRECTIONS

- Bring water and a dash of table salt to a boil in a small saucepan.
- Oats should be added after reducing heat to medium and cooking for about 5 minutes while stirring occasionally.
- Withdraw from heat, cover, and let stand for two to three minutes.
- Add a banana, chocolate spread, and salt flake on top.

Egg Salad Avocado Toast

Nutrition Facts (Per serving) Calories 230 Fat 13.7g Sodium 405g Carbs 17.2g Protein 10.8g Potassium 400 mg Phosphorus 173g

Prep time: 5 minutes Total time: 5 minutes Serving Size 1 serving

Quite a morning? Try out this 5-minute, nutritious, quick, and tasty breakfast.

INGREDIENTS

¼ avocado •1 tablespoon of celery •½ teaspoon of lemon juice •½ teaspoon of spicy sauce •A dash of salt •A single diced hard-boiled egg •1 piece of Whole-wheat bread

DIRECTIONS

- In a small bowl, mash avocado with celery, lemon juice, spicy sauce, and salt.
- Add the hard-boiled egg and combine.
- Apply to toast.

Maple-Nut Granola

Nutrition Facts (Per serving) Calories 242 Fat 12g Sodium 6g Carbs 31.4g Protein 4.8g Potassium 209 mg Phosphorus 165g

Prep time: 10 minutes Total time: 1 hour 40 minutes Serving size 10 cups

INGREDIENTS

5 cups of traditional rolled oats •1 cup of coconut flakes or chips without added sugar •Sliced almonds in a cup •½ cup pecans, roughly chopped •½ cup of light brown sugar •⅓ Unsalted pumpkin seeds •⅓ Unsalted sunflower seeds •½ cups of pure maple syrup •½ cup of water •¼ Canola oil •½ ounces of dried cranberries •½ cup of raisins

DIRECTIONS

- Set the oven to 275°F.
- In a large bowl, mix the oats, coconut, almonds, pecans, brown sugar, pumpkin seeds, and sunflower seeds.
- Pour the syrup, water, and oil into a medium bowl or large measuring cup and blend before adding the oat mixture.
- Spread the mixture onto a large (12 by 15 inch) rimmed baking sheet or roasting pan.
- For 45 minutes, bake. Then, bake for another 45 minutes or more, stirring occasionally, until crisp and golden brown.
- Add the raisins and cranberries.
- Allow to fully cool before storing.

Maple Granola

Nutrition Facts (Per Serving) Calories 147 Fat 7.8g Sodium 50g Carbs 17.7g Protein 2.7g Potassium 102 mg Phosphorus 82g

Prep time: 10 minutes Total time: 25 minutes Serving size 5 servings

This simple and healthful granola recipe may be used to create a quick parfait or eaten as cereal with milk. For a well-rounded breakfast, serve with a banana

INGREDIENTS

2 teaspoons of pure maple syrup •1 tablespoon of Canola oil •¼ teaspoon of vanilla •1 cup of rolled oats •¼ cup of Pecans, chopped •1 ½ teaspoons of cinnamon powder •⅛ teaspoon of kosher salt

DIRECTIONS

- Set the oven to 325°F. A baking sheet with a rim should be lined with parchment paper.
- In a medium bowl, mix the oil, vanilla, and maple syrup. Oats, pecans, cinnamon, and salt are added and mixed well.
- On the prepared baking sheet, evenly distribute it.
- Granola should be baked for 10 to 15 minutes, stirring halfway through, until brown.
- Allow to fully cool before storing.

Salsa Scrambled Eggs

Nutrition Facts (Per serving) Calories 279 Fat 13g Sodium 320g Carbs 23.3g Protein 17.3g Potassium 279 mg Phosphorus 386g

Prep time: 10 minutes Total time: 10 minutes Serving size 1 servings

Breakfast tacos are a fantastic gluten-free substitute for traditional eggs and toast. Give this simple scrambled egg dish a potassium boost by serving it with a banana.

INGREDIENTS

2 big eggs •1 tablespoon of Jack cheese, shredded •1 tablespoon salsa fraîche •2 warmed corn tortillas •Fresh cilantro, 1 teaspoon

DIRECTIONS

- In a basin, beat the eggs. Cooking spray should be used to coat a small nonstick pan before heating it up.
- Add the eggs and whisk while cooking until almost set.
- Mix thoroughly after adding the cheese and salsa.
- Top with cilantro after spooning into tortillas.

Apple Oatmeal

Nutrition Facts (Per Serving) Calories 211 Fat 1.6g Sodium 167g Carbs 45.7g Protein 6g Potassium 275 mg Phosphorus 139g

Prep time: 45 minutes Total time: 45 minutes Serving size 5 cups

Cooking apples into your morning oatmeal with this nutritious recipe will give you a portion of fruit and whole grains to start the day off well.

INGREDIENTS

4 crisp apples, such as Pink Lady or Jazz, chopped •1 cup of steel-cut oats •4 cups of Water •3 teaspoons of divided, packed brown sugar •½ teaspoons of cinnamon powder •¼ grains of salt •½ cups of plain, nonfat Greek yogurt

DIRECTIONS

- Using a box grater with big holes, shred two apples, leaving the core behind.
- Large saucepan heated to a medium-high temperature.
- Oats should be added and cooked for approximately two minutes while stirring constantly.
- Bring the shredded apples, water, and salt to a boil.
- Cook for 10 minutes, stirring often, over low heat to maintain a simmer.
- Chop the remaining 2 apples in the meanwhile.
- After the oats have simmered for 10 minutes, add the chopped apples, 2 tablespoons brown sugar, cinnamon, and salt.

- Cook the mixture, stirring regularly, for an additional 15 to 20 minutes, or until the apples are soft and the oatmeal is rather thick.
- Oatmeal is divided among four dishes.
- Add two tablespoons of yogurt and one-third of a teaspoon of brown sugar to each serving.

Old- Fashioned Oatmeal

Nutrition Facts (Per Serving) Calories 154 Fat 2.6g Sodium 155g Carbs 27.4g Protein 5.3g Potassium 149 mg Phosphorus 166g

Prep time: 15 minutes Total time: 15 minutes Serving size 1 cup

Old-fashioned oatmeal may be cooked for only a few more minutes before becoming extra-creamy and decadent, unlike quick-cooking oats. Old-fashioned oats may be your go-to breakfast option for hearty, substantial meals in the morning when combined with a little milk and your preferred toppings.

INGREDIENTS

1 cup of low-fat milk or water plus an additional 1 ounce of milk per serving •A dash of Salt •½ cups of rolled oats •1 to 2 tablespoons of optional honey, cane sugar, or brown sugar •A pinch of Cinnamon

DIRECTIONS

- **Using a Stovetop**: Combine salt, water (or one cup of milk), and a small saucepan. up to a boil.
- Oats are added once the heat is reduced to medium.
- Cook for 5 minutes while stirring periodically.
- Turn off the heat, cover the pan, and let it rest for two to three minutes.
- **Using the Microwave**: In a 2-cup dish, mix the salt, water (or 1 cup of milk), and oats. 2-4 minutes on High in a microwave.
- Before serving, stir.
- If preferred, add milk, sweetener, cinnamon, dried fruit, or nuts to the top.

Southwest Baked Egg Breakfast

Nutrition Facts (Per Serving) Calories 109 Fat 4g Sodium 79g Carbs 13g Protein 5g Potassium 82mg Phosphorus 91g

Prep time: 5 minutes Total time: 20minutes Serving size : 1 egg cup or 2.5 ounces.

These baked morning egg cups will jolt your taste buds with their delicious rice, eggs, green chiles, pimentos, and cheddar cheese filling. A delectable way to start the day

INGREDIENTS

3 cups of cooked rice •4 ounces of shredded cheddar cheese •4 diced ounces of green chili •2 ounces of chopped and drained pimentos •½ cup skim milk •2 beaten eggs •½ teaspoon cumin powder •½ teaspoons of black pepper •Cookware nonstick spray

DIRECTIONS

- Rice, 2 ounces of cheese, milk, eggs, chiles, pimentos, cumin, and pepper should all be combined in a big dish.
- Spray nonstick cooking spray onto muffin tins.
- Spread the mixture evenly among the 12 muffin tins. Top up each cup with the final 2 ounces of cheese shavings.

Fuel up with a nutritious, delicious lunch!

LUNCH RECIPES

Egg Fried Rice

Crunchy Quinoa Salad

Mediterranean Green Beans

Mexican Pasta Salad with Creamy Avocado Dressing

Creamy Coleslaw

Hawaiian Turkey Sliders

Brussels Sprouts Chips

Margherita Pizza

Chili Cornbread Casserole

Pumpkin Strudel

Egg Fried Rice

Nutrition Facts (Per Serving) Calories 137 Fat 4g Carbs 21g Protein 5g Potassium 89 mg Phosphorus 67g

Prep time: 10 minutes Total time: 10 minutes Serves 10 (1 serving = ½ cup)

A tasty, quick Asian-inspired dinner for individuals who are always on the go This egg fried rice dish mixes scrambled eggs, rice, green onions, peas, and bean sprouts to make a hearty and delightful vegetarian supper.

INGREDIENTS

2 tsp. dark sesame oil •2 eggs •2 beaten egg whites •1 teaspoon of canola oil •1 cup sprouted beans •⅓ cup chopped green onions •4 cups cold cooked rice •1 cup thawed frozen peas •¼ teaspoon black pepper, ground.

DIRECTIONS

- In a small mixing dish, combine the sesame oil, eggs, and egg whites. Set aside after thoroughly mixing.
- In a large nonstick skillet over medium-high heat, heat the canola oil.
- Stir in the egg mixture until it is done.
- Mix in the bean sprouts and green onions. 2 minutes of stirring
- Mix in the rice and peas. Continue to stir-fry until completely hot.
- Serve immediately after seasoning with black pepper.

Crunchy Quinoa Salad

Nutrition Facts (Per Serving) Calories 158 Fat 9g Sodium 46g Carbs 16g Protein 5g Potassium 237 mg Phosphorus 129g

Prep time: 5 minutes Total time: 20 minutes Serving size 1 cup

The nutty flavor of protein-packed quinoa is combined with tomatoes, cucumbers, green onions, fresh mint, and parsley in this crisp, colorful quinoa salad. Pour the salad into Bibb lettuce leaf "cups" for an extra cool crunch.

INGREDIENTS

1 cup of washed quinoa •2 cups of water •5 diced cherry tomatoes •½ cup seeded and sliced cucumbers •3 chopped green onions •¼ cup chopped fresh mint •½ cups of chopped flat-leaf parsley •2 tablespoons of fresh lemon juice •1 tablespoon of lemon zest (grated) •4 tablespoons of olive oil •¼ cup grated parmesan cheese •½ heads of Boston or Bibb lettuce, divided into cups

DIRECTIONS

- Rinse the quinoa under cold running water until it is clear, then drain well.
- Toast the quinoa in a skillet over medium-high heat for 2 minutes, turning constantly. Bring to a boil with 2 cups of water. Reduce the heat to low, cover the pan, and leave to cook for 8–10 minutes.
- Allow to cook before fluffing with a fork.
- Combine the herbs, lemon juice, zest, and olive oil with the tomatoes, cucumbers, and onions. To the mixture, add the chilled quinoa.
- Spoon the mixture into lettuce cups and top with parmesan cheese.

Mediterranean Green Beans

Nutrition Facts (Per Serving) Calories 71 Fat 3g Sodium 2g Carbs 10g Protein 2g Potassium 186 mg Phosphorus 37g

Prep time: 10 minutes Total time: 10 minutes Serving size 1 cup

Simply delectable. Green beans in an olive oil, fresh minced garlic, lemon juice, and ground pepper dressing

INGREDIENTS

1 pound of fresh green beans, cut into 1- to 2-inch pieces •¾ cups of water •2 ½ tablespoons olive oil•3 minced fresh garlic cloves •3 tbsp. fresh lemon juice •1/8 teaspoon black pepper, ground

DIRECTIONS

- In a large nonstick skillet, bring water to a boil; add beans and cook for 3 minutes; drain and put aside.
- Heat the oil in a pan over medium-high heat; add the garlic and beans and cook for 1 minute.
- Cook for 1 minute more after adding the juice and pepper.

TIP: To bring out the flavors in food, use lemon juice instead of salt.

Mexican Pasta Salad with Creamy Avocado Dressing

Nutrition Facts (Per Serving) Calories 297 Fat 13.3g Sodium 349g Carbs 37.9g Protein 10.1g Potassium 346 mg Phosphorus 193g

Prep time: 20 minutes Total time: 20 minutes Serving size 1 cup

It's impossible to go wrong with this recipe for pasta salad with Mexican flavors. For a healthy take on a picnic staple, we add avocado to the creamy dressing to lighten it up.

INGREDIENTS

Dressing

½ avocado •¼ cup of Mayonnaise •2 tbsp lime juice •1 tiny clove of grated garlic •½ teaspoons of salt •¼ tsp. cumin

Pasta salad

8 ounces (3 cups) of whole-wheat fusilli •1 cup cherry or grape tomatoes, halved •½ cups drained black beans from cans •½ cups fresh or frozen (thawed) corn •½ cups shredded Cheddar cheese •¼ cup red onion, chopped •¼ cup fresh cilantro, chopped

DIRECTIONS

- **How to make dressing In a small food processor:** Combine the avocado, mayonnaise, lime juice, garlic, salt, and cumin. until smooth, puree.

- **Making pasta salad**: In a big pot of boiling water, cook pasta as directed on the package. After washing with cold water, drain one more time.

- Place it in a large bowl. Tomatoes, beans, corn, Cheddar, onion, and cilantro are stirred in.

- Dressing added; toss to coat.

Tips: Without dressing, cover and store in the fridge for up to a day.

About an hour before serving, toss with the dressing.

Creamy Coleslaw

Nutrition Facts (Per Serving) Calories 48 Fat 1.5g Sodium 171g Carbs 8g Protein 1.4g Potassium 181 mg Phosphorus 35g

Prep time: 20 minutes Total time: 20 minutes Serving size 6 servings

A vivid and healthy blend of carrots in a vibrant orange color with red, green, and white cabbage Savoy green cabbage has a more nutty flavor than typical green cabbage.

INGREDIENTS

3 tablespoons of low-fat mayo •3 tablespoons plain nonfat yogurt •1 tablespoon of Dijon mustard •2-teaspoons of cider vinegar •1 teaspoon of sugar •½ teaspoons celery or caraway seeds, if desired •To improve the flavor, season with salt and pepper •1/4 of a small bunch of red cabbage, 2 cups of shredded •1/4 of a small head of green cabbage, 2 cups of finely chopped •2 medium-sized shredded carrots, 1 cup

DIRECTIONS

- In a big bowl, mix mayo, yogurt, mustard, vinegar, and sugar.(If using, add the caraway (or celery) seed.)
- Add salt and pepper to taste. Stir in the cabbage and carrots.

Hawaiian Turkey Sliders

Nutrition Facts (Per Serving) Calories 286 Fat 11.3g Sodium 368g Carbs 28.1g Protein 18.7g Potassium 325 mg Phosphorus 205g

Prep time: 30 minutes Total time: 30 minutes Serving size 6 sliders

The savory turkey burgers on these simple sliders are topped with grilled pineapple for a Hawaiian twist.

INGREDIENTS

1 pound of 93% lean ground turkey •2 tablespoons of teriyaki sauce with less sodium •2 sliced scallions •1 big clove of minced garlic •6 1/4-inch-thick fresh pineapple rings •1 tiny red onion, sliced into rings that are 1/4 inch thick •6 whole-wheat, lightly toasted slider buns •2 tablespoons of mayo •6 small leaves of Boston lettuce

DIRECTIONS

- Set the grill to medium-high heat.
- In a medium bowl, mix the turkey, teriyaki sauce, scallions, and garlic. Gently knead the mixture.
- Avoid overmixing.
- Make six 3-inch-wide burgers using the mixture.
- Grill the burgers for 2 to 3 minutes on each side, or until an instant-read thermometer placed in the middle reads 165°F.
- Grill pineapple rings for 2 minutes on each side, or until just barely browned.
- Add 1 teaspoon mayonnaise, 1 lettuce leaf, 1 pineapple ring, and around 3 onion rings to each burger before assembling it on a toasted bun.

Brussels Sprouts Chips

Nutrition Facts (Per Serving) Calories 41 Fat 3.6g Sodium 78g Carbs 2g Protein 0.7g Potassium 85 mg Phosphorus 15g

Prep time: 10 minutes Total time: 20 minutes Serving size 2 cups

These Brussels sprout chips will be to your taste if you enjoy kale chips. The outer leaves of Brussels sprouts are baked in the oven for about 10 minutes using this 4-ingredient recipe to make a nutritious snack. But save the insides of the sprouts; they make a delicious side dish when roasted.

INGREDIENTS

About 15 medium-sized Brussels sprouts •1 tablespoon of extra virgin olive oil •¼ teaspoon of pepper, ground •⅛ teaspoons of salt

DIRECTIONS

- Set the oven to 400 °F.
- Remove enough Brussels sprouts outer leaves to yield 4 cups.
- Put it in a big bowl and season with salt, pepper, and oil.
- Gently rub the leaves with clean hands until they are covered all over.
- On a large baking sheet with a rim, spread it out in a single layer.
- About 10 minutes of roasting are required to get the leaves crispy and caramelized.

Margherita Pizza

Nutrition Facts (Per Serving) Calories 41 Fat 3.6g Sodium 78g Carbs 2g Protein 0.7g Potassium 85 mg Phosphorus 15g

Prep time: 10 minutes Total time: 25 minutes Serving size 5 servings

It just takes 25 minutes to prepare this delicious Margherita pizza recipe. Pre-made pizza dough is transformed into the ideal quick family supper with the aid of creamy mozzarella and fresh basil leaves.

INGREDIENTS

Packed dough with a thin crust (no additives) a prepared crust •1 tablespoon of olive oil •¼ to ½ cup of chunky tomato sauce (use a 28-ounce can of whole, crushed tomatoes) •(Optional) ¼ tsp. garlic powder •1 inch mozzarella balls packaged in a package •Choose your own seasonings and fresh basil (5–6 basil leaves).

DIRECTIONS

- The crust may be baked to brown or toasted.
- Lightly brush the crust with virgin olive oil.
- Over olive oil, spread sauce on the crust.
- Share 10 mozzarella balls to the pizza.
- 10 minutes of pizza baking at 450°
- Add fresh basil and spices to the mix
- Drizzle some olive oil.

Chili Cornbread Casserole

Nutrition Facts (Per Serving) Calories 392 Fat 21g Sodium 335g Carbs 33g Protein 17g Potassium 441 mg Phosphorus 239g

Prep time: 20 minutes Total time: 60 minutes Serving size 1 serving

This dish blends rich chili with moist cornbread to make a mouthwatering feast that your family and guests won't soon forget.

INGREDIENTS

For Chili

1 pound of ground beef •½ cups diced onions •¼ cup diced celery •2 teaspoons finely chopped jalapenos •½ cups chopped red or green peppers •A teaspoon of chili powder •1 tablespoon of granulated garlic powder •2 teaspoons of flakes of dried onion •1 teaspoon of cumin •1 teaspoon of black pepper, ground •½ cups tomato sauce with no salt added •¼ cup of water •¼ cup of the reduced sodium French's® Worcestershire sauce •1 cup of washed and drained kidney beans •1 cup of shredded cheddar cheese

For Cornbread

¼ cup cornmeal •¾ cup of flour •¼ tsp. baking soda •½ tsp. cream of tartar •½ cups of sugar •1 beaten egg •1½ tablespoons of salted , melted butter •¼ cup of Canola oil •¾ cups of milk

DIRECTIONS

- In a large saucepan, combine the brown ground beef with the onions, celery, jalapenos, and bell peppers. Excess oil should be drained. Add the chili powder, garlic powder, onion flakes, cumin, black pepper, tomato sauce, water, Worcestershire sauce, and beans.

- Cook for an additional 10 minutes.

- Remove from heat and pour into a 9" x 9" baking pan, then cover with cheese.

- In a medium mixing bowl, combine cornmeal, flour, baking soda, cream of tartar, and sugar.

- In a small bowl, combine the egg, melted butter, oil, and milk.

- Fold the flour mixture and egg mixture together (some lumps are okay; don't overbeat).
- Pour the mixture over the chili and bake for 25 minutes uncovered, then 20 minutes covered at 350° F, then turn off the oven and allow it to rest for 5 minutes.

Pumpkin Strudel

Nutrition Facts (Per Serving) Calories 180 Fat 8g Sodium 141g Carbs 25g Protein 3g Potassium 119 mg Phosphorus 39g.

Prep time: 20 minutes Total time: 45 minutes Serving size 1 serving (1 slice)

With the pumpkin filling enveloped in crispy phyllo pastry, this toasted strudel is the ideal take on pumpkin pie. It's loaded with sugar, spices, and everything lovely for lunch. With the pumpkin filling enveloped in crispy phyllo pastry, this toasted strudel is the ideal take on pumpkin pie. It's loaded with sugar, spices, and everything lovely for a holiday dessert.

INGREDIENTS

1½ cups canned unsweetened pumpkin, sodium-free •⅛ teaspoon of grated nutmeg •1 teaspoon pure vanilla extract •4 tablespoons of sugar •½ teaspoons of Cinnamon powder •1/2 sticks (4 tablespoons) unsalted,melted butter •12 sheets phyllo dough (if frozen, thaw according to package recommendations)

DIRECTIONS

- The oven rack should be positioned in the middle of the oven. Preheat the oven to 375 ° F.
- Combine the canned pumpkin, nutmeg, vanilla essence, 2 tablespoons sugar, and 1/2 teaspoons cinnamon in a medium-sized mixing dish.
- Coat the bottom of a nonstick medium sheet tray with melted butter using a pastry brush. Lay out a single sheet of phyllo dough on a clean work area and brush it with butter.
- Then make a stack of buttered phyllo sheets, brushing each one with butter.

- (Reserve a little melted butter to brush the top of the rolled-filled strudel, so brush softly in between layers.) Cover the leftover phyllo dough sheets with plastic wrap until ready to use so as to prevent them from drying out.

- When all 12 sheets have been utilized, pour the mixture equally along one of the stack's long edges. Roll from the filled end to the empty end, seam side down.

- Transfer the roll to the prepared sheet tray, seam side down, and brush with the remaining butter.

- In a separate dish, combine the remaining sugar and cinnamon.

- Sprinkle it on the strudel's top and sides.

- Bake for 12–15 minutes on the center rack, or until gently toasted or golden brown.

- Remove the toasted strudel from the oven and leave aside for 5–10 minutes before slicing with a sharp knife to enable the center to settle.

- Serve

Savor every bite of a kidney-friendly dinner!

DINNER RECIPES

Spaghetti and Asparagus Carbonara

Mashed Carrots & Ginger

Sautéed Collard Greens

Fish Tacos with Avocado-Lime Crema

Stuffed Avocados

Stuffed Delicata Squash

Easy Brown Rice

Easy Fried Rice

Greek Stuffed Portobello Mushrooms

Sweet and Crunchy Coleslaw

Vinegary Coleslaw

Roasted Broccoli with Lemon

Spicy Tofu Scrambler

Spinach & Strawberry Salad with Poppy Seed Dressing

Spaghetti and Asparagus Carbonara

Nutrition Facts (Per Serving) Calories 304 Fat 19g Sodium 141g Carbs 27g Protein 9g Potassium 287 mg Phosphorus 143g

Prep time: 15 minutes Total time: 20 minutes Serving size 1 serving (1 cup)

This flavorful pasta recipe is quick and simple to prepare and offers a filling supper. Salmon or chicken can be added for more protein.

INGREDIENTS

2 teaspoons of canola oil •1 cup diced fresh onions •1 big egg, beaten •1 cup of heavy cream •¼ cup of chicken stock low in salt •3 cups of cooked, al dente spiral noodle pasta (about 1 ½ cups raw) •2 cups chopped, 1-inch-long segments of fresh asparagus •1 teaspoon of freshly cracked black pepper, coarse •1⁄2 cup of finely chopped fresh scallions •3 teaspoons of meatless bacon bits •3 teaspoons of shredded Parmesan cheese

DIRECTIONS

- Oil should be heated in a large nonstick sauté pan over medium-high heat before the onions are sautéed and nicely browned.

- In the meantime, combine the egg and cream completely in a small dish.

- When the cream mixture begins to thicken, about 4 to 6 minutes, reduce the heat to medium-low and pour it into the onions while swirling frequently with a wooden spoon.

- Continue to stir for an additional 3–4 minutes or until well heated before adding the stock, pasta, asparagus, and black pepper.

- In a serving dish, pour the carbonara after turning off the heat.

- Serve garnished with cheese, scallions, and bacon pieces.

Mashed Carrots and Ginger

Nutrition Facts (Per Serving) Calories 30 Fat 0g Sodium 281g Carbs 7g Protein 1g Potassium 174 mg Phosphorus 21g

Prep time: 5 minutes Total time: 15 minutes Serving size 1 serving (1/3)

This traditional side dish for the holidays will add color and flavor to your dinner table. Ginger, honey, black pepper, and a tiny bit of vanilla essence are added to the seasoning for mashed carrots. A colorful and velvety meal that couldn't be easier to make—or taste better.

INGREDIENTS

Two cups of baby carrots •½ teaspoons of finely chopped fresh ginger •½ tsp. of honey •½ tsp. of black pepper •½ tsp. vanilla extract •One tablespoon of chopped fresh chives is an optional garnish.

DIRECTIONS

- Carrots should be boiled or steam-cooked over high heat until extremely soft. Utilizing a potato masher, turn the heat to low and mash the carrots.
- Ginger, honey, pepper, and vanilla essence are added next. Stir everything together until completely combined.

The serving size is three, or one-third of the recipe.

Optional: Serve after adding chopped chives as a garnish.

TIP: Use a food processor or blender to mix the carrots into a smoother consistency.

Sautéed Collard Greens

Nutrition Facts (Per Serving) Calories 79 Fat 7g Sodium 9g Carbs 4g Protein 2g Potassium 129 mg Phosphorus 18g

Prep time: 15 minutes Total time: 15 minutes Serving size 1 serving (1/6 portion)

This simple collard greens recipe is a tasty and healthful veggie side dish for dinner.

INGREDIENTS

8 cups blanched and sliced fresh collard greens •2 tbsp olive oil •1 tablespoon of unsalted butter •¼ cup of diced onions •1 tablespoon chopped fresh garlic •1 teaspoon crushed red pepper flakes •1 teaspoon ground black pepper •1 tablespoon vinegar (optional)

DIRECTIONS

- Put the collard greens in a saucepan of boiling water for 30 seconds to blanch them.
- Remove the greens from the boiling water with a strainer, then rapidly place them in a big dish of cool water.
- Let the greens cool, then filter, dry, and set them aside.
- Heat the butter and oil to medium-high in a large sauté pan.
- Add the onions and garlic and simmer for 4–6 minutes, until they start to turn somewhat brown.
- Black and red peppers are then added, and the collard greens are cooked for 5-8 minutes over high heat while being regularly stirred.
- Remove from heat, add vinegar if desired, and mix.

Fish Tacos with Avocado-Lime Crema

Nutrition Facts (Per Serving) Calories 395 Fat 23.8g Sodium 416g Carbs 38.1g Protein. 9.7g Potassium 402 mg Phosphorus 279g

Prep time: 15 minutes Total time: 30 minutes Serving size 8 tacos

In this healthy meal recipe, frozen fish sticks are your fish taco rescuer if battering and frying fish looks messy. Try popcorn shrimp or use them as a fast, kid-friendly supper. Serve with black beans on the side and your preferred salsa.

INGREDIENTS

8 ounces or 16 fish sticks •3 cups of shredded cabbage or coleslaw mix •Rice vinegar, two teaspoons •⅛ grains of salt •½ ripe avocado •¼ cup of Mayonnaise •2 tablespoons of lime juice •½ tsp. of spicy sauce •8 warmed corn tortillas •Citrus as a garnish

DIRECTIONS

- Follow the instructions on the box to prepare fish sticks.

- Mix the coleslaw mix (or cabbage) with the vinegar and salt in the meantime.

- Mayonnaise, lime juice, and spicy sauce should all be combined with mashed avocado in a small bowl.

- If desired, top the fish sticks in tortillas with cilantro, avocado crema, and slaw.

Stuffed Avocados

Nutrition Facts (Per Serving) Calories 174 Fat 11.7g Sodium 223g Carbs 7.2g Protein 11.8g Potassium 554 mg Phosphorus 128g

Prep time: 20 minutes Total time: 20 minutes Serving size 5 servings

A light, creamy dressing with pimientos and a dash of pepper enhances a sumptuous yet healthy fish salad. Avocado halves may be stuffed with it to make a delicious lunch or light dinner.

INGREDIENTS

¼ cup plain nonfat yogurt •2 teaspoons of low-fat mayo •2 teaspoons of washed and dried pimientos •1 minced tiny clove of garlic •⅛ teaspoon of Cayenne pepper, or to your preferred taste •⅛ teaspoon of Salt or to taste •2⅔ cups cooked crab flesh, trimmed •2 halved ripe avocados •Slices of lemon as a garnish

DIRECTIONS

- In a blender, combine the yogurt, mayonnaise, pimientos, garlic, cayenne, and salt.
- Until smooth, blend.
- Add crab after transferring to a bowl.
- Add salt and pepper to taste.
- Among the avocado halves, divide the crab salad.
- Lemon wedges are recommended.

Stuffed Delicata Squash

Nutrition Facts (Per Serving) Calories 319 Fat 8.7g Sodium 481g Carbs 34.8g Protein 17.7g Potassium 843 mg Phosphorus 280g

Prep time: 40 minutes Total time: 40 minutes Serving size 4 stuffed squash halves

To minimize saturated fat without sacrificing the amount of filling, we substitute half of the ground beef you would typically use for bulgur in this Tex-Mex-seasoned stuffed delicata squash dish. Serve alongside a salad of mixed greens with a cilantro vinaigrette.

INGREDIENTS

2 small delicata squash, cut in half and seeded (each weighs around 12 ounces). •Extra virgin olive oil, divided into 6 teaspoons •½ teaspoon salt, split •½ cups of bulgur •1 cup of water •1 minced tiny onion •8 ounces of 90% or leaner ground beef •2 teaspoons of Chili powder •½ cup plain yogurt that is nonfat or low-fat •4 tablespoons lightly toast pepitas

DIRECTIONS

- Oven should be heated to 425°F.
- Sprinkle 1/4 teaspoon salt and two tablespoons of oil on the squash's sliced sides.
- On a large baking sheet, position face down. 25 to 30 minutes of baking time will result in tender and browned edges.
- In the meantime, heat water and bulgur to a boil in a small pot.
- Simmer for approximately 10 minutes, or until the vegetables are soft and most of the liquid has been absorbed.
- Do a good job of draining.

- In a big skillet over medium heat, heat the remaining 4 teaspoons of oil.
- Add the onion and stir until it starts to brown, about 4 to 5 minutes. Add the beef, chili powder, and remaining 1/4 teaspoon salt. Cook, turning occasionally, for approximately 5 minutes, or until the meat is well cooked. Bulgur is added and heated for one minute. Add yogurt and stir.
- Fill each squash half with about 3/4 cup of the filling.
- Serve with pepitas on top.

Easy Brown Rice

Nutrition Facts (Per Serving) Calories 113 Fat 1g Sodium 4g Carbs 23.5g Protein 2.3g Potassium 78 mg Phosphorus 96g

Prep time: 5 minutes Total time: 1 hr Serving size 6 servings

You only need this one recipe to consistently create beautiful brown rice!

Use this nutritious whole grain in your favorite recipes that call for cooked brown rice or enjoy it on its own as a side dish.

INGREDIENTS

2½ cups of broth or water •1 cup of brown rice

DIRECTIONS

- In a medium pot, add rice and water (or broth). up to a boil.
- Reduce heat to low, cover, and simmer for 40 to 50 minutes, or until the vegetables are soft and most of the liquid has been absorbed.
- Five minutes of standing time is followed by fork fluffing.

Easy Fried Rice

Nutrition Facts (Per Serving) Calories 137 Fat 4g Sodium 38g Carbs 21g Protein 5g Potassium 89 mg Phosphorus 67g

Prep time: 10 minutes Total time: 10 minutes Serving size 10 servings(1 serving = ½ cup)

For a tasty, simple-to-make meal with Asian influences for folks who are constantly on the go for a hearty and fulfilling vegetarian supper, try this recipe for egg fried rice, which mixes scrambled eggs, rice, green onions, peas, and bean sprouts.

INGREDIENTS

2 tablespoons of dark sesame oil •2 eggs •2-egg whites •1 tsp. of canola oil •1 cup of bean sprouts •⅓ cups of finely chopped green onions •4 cups of chilled, cooked rice •1 cup defrosted frozen peas •1⁄4 teaspoon of freshly ground pepper

DIRECTIONS

- In a small bowl, mix the egg yolks, egg whites, and sesame oil.
- Stir thoroughly, then pause.
- In a large nonstick skillet set over medium-high heat, heat canola oil.
- Stir-fry until you are finished adding the egg mixture.
- Put in bean sprouts and green onions. For two minutes, stir-fry.
- Rice and peas should be added. Stir-frying should continue until everything is hot.
- Serve soon after adding black pepper to the food.

Greek Stuffed Portobello Mushrooms

Nutrition Facts (Per Serving) Calories 114 Fat 8.5g Sodium 390g Carbs 6.6g Protein 4.5g Potassium 467 mg Phosphorus 159g

Prep time: 15 minutes Total time: 25 minutes Serving size 4 stuffed mushrooms

This nutritious stuffed mushroom dish imbues portobellos with a Mediterranean flavor thanks to a combination of tomatoes, spinach, feta, olives, and fresh oregano. Serve them as a filling side dish with chicken, fish, or tofu, or use them as the main course of a vegetarian supper by incorporating them into a robust salad.

INGREDIENTS

3 tablespoons of extra virgin olive oil, split •1 minced garlic clove •½ teaspoons split of ground pepper •¼ teaspoons of salt •4 cleaned, gills removed, and around 14 ounces of portobello mushrooms •1 cup of spinach, chopped •½ cups of cherry tomatoes, quartered •1/3 cup feta cheese crumbles •2 tablespoons of Kalamata olives, pitted and sliced •1 tablespoon freshly chopped oregano

DIRECTIONS

- Preheat the oven to 400°F.
- In a small dish, mix 2 tablespoons of oil, 1/8 teaspoon each of salt and pepper, and the garlic.
- Apply the oil mixture all over the mushrooms using a silicone brush.
- Place the mushrooms on a large baking sheet with a rim and bake for 8 to 10 minutes, or until mostly soft.
- In the meantime, mix the remaining 1 tablespoon oil, spinach, tomatoes, feta, olives, and oregano in a medium bowl.
- Remove the mushrooms from the oven after they have softened, then fill them with the spinach mixture.
- About 10 minutes into baking, the tomatoes should be wilted.

Sweet and Crunchy Coleslaw

Nutrition Facts (Per Serving) Calories 244 Fat 19g Sodium 12g Carbs 20g Protein 1g Potassium 73mg Phosphorus 13g

Prep time: 10 minutes Total time: 10 minutes Serving size 12 serving (1 serving = ½ cup)

This unique take on traditional coleslaw is flavorful and crunchy because of the sweet onion, celery seed, and a splash of mustard. Give it as a side dish for supper or lunch.

INGREDIENTS

6 cups of cabbage shreds •½ cups of chopped sweet onions •1 cup of sugar •1 cup of canola oil •1 tsp. celery seeds •½ cups of rice vinegar •1 teaspoon prepared yellow mustard

DIRECTIONS

- In a big bowl, combine the chopped onion and cabbage.
- Blend the remaining ingredients in a blender until fully blended.
- Over the onion and cabbage, pour the dressing.
- Stir thoroughly, then chill.
- Serve chilled.

Vinegary Coleslaw

Nutrition Facts (Per Serving) Calories 104 Fat 7.2g Sodium 137 g Carbs 10g Protein 1.2g Potassium 217 mg Phosphorus 30g

Prep time: 10 minutes Total time: 10 minutes Serving size 2 servings (1 cup each)

Leave the mayonnaise-heavy coleslaw at home. Everything from tacos to barbeque benefits from the fresh, crisp tastes in this rendition.

INGREDIENTS

1 teaspoon white-wine vinegar •1 teaspoon of canola oil •1 teaspoon of sugar •1 teaspoon of Dijon mustard •1 pinch of celery seed •A dash of salt •1 ½ cups of shredded cabbage •1 peeled and grated carrot •1/4 cup shaved red onion

DIRECTIONS

- In a medium bowl, combine the salt, celery seed, mustard, oil, and vinegar.
- Combine the cabbage, onion, and carrot.
- Serve.

Roasted Broccoli with Lemon

Nutrition Facts (Per Serving) Calories 54 Fat 3.8g Sodium 165g Carbs 4.3g Protein 2.2g Potassium 241 mg Phosphorus 48g

Prep time: 10 minutes Total time: 15 minutes Serving size 4 servings (1 cup each)

Perhaps roasting broccoli has never occurred to you, yet it produces unexpectedly tasty results. The natural sugars are caramelized, and the tastes are concentrated by the heat. It has a crunchy, wonderful finish and a small amount of olive oil.

INGREDIENTS

4 cups of broccoli florets •1 tablespoon virgin olive •1/4 teaspoon of salt •Freshly ground pepper •Lemon slices

DIRECTIONS

- Preheat the oven to 450°F.
- Combine oil, salt, and pepper with the broccoli.
- Place on a large, non-insulated baking sheet and roast for 10 to 12 minutes, or until the bottom of the broccoli is browned and soft.
- Serve immediately with lemon wedges.

Spicy Tofu Scrambler

Nutrition Facts (Per Serving) Calories 223 Fat 13g Sodium 24g Carbs 10g Protein 18g Potassium 467 mg Phosphorus 242g

Prep time: 10 minutes Total time: 30 minutes Serving size 2 servings (1 serving = ½ cup)

This vegan, protein-packed tofu scrambler creates a delicious alternative for breakfast thanks to a combination of spices and vegetables. The eggs won't even be missed!

INGREDIENTS

1 teaspoon of olive oil •1/4 cup finely minced red bell pepper •1/4 cup chopped green bell pepper •One cup of firm tofu (less than 10% calcium is preferred) •1 teaspoon of powdered onion •1/4 teaspoon garlic powder •1 minced garlic clove•1/8 teaspoon of turmeric

DIRECTIONS

- Garlic and both bell peppers should be sautéed in olive oil in a medium-sized non-stick pan.
- Tofu should be rinsed, drained, and crumbled into the pan.
- Include the remaining components.
- For about 20 minutes, stir and cook the tofu on low to medium heat until it turns a light golden brown.
- The mixture will lose water through evaporation.
- Serve heated tofu scrambles.

Spinach & Strawberry Salad with Poppy Seed Dressing

Nutrition Facts (Per Serving) Calories 148 Fat 13.4g Sodium 290g Carbs 4.8g Protein 2.5g Potassium 169 mg Phosphorus 65g

Prep time: 20 minutes Total time: 20 minutes Serving size 6 servings

For a deliciously light and simple spring salad, combine delicate spinach, crisp almonds, and luscious berries with homemade poppy seed dressing.
Add some shrimp or chicken that has been grilled to make it a full dinner.

INGREDIENTS

2½ tablespoons of mayonnaise •1 ½ teaspoons apple cider vinegar •Extra virgin olive oil, 1 tablespoon •1 teaspoon of poppy seeds •1 teaspoon of sugar •1/4 teaspoon of salt •1/4 teaspoon of pepper, ground •1 package of baby spinach, 5 ounces •1 cup of strawberry slices •1/4 cup of sliced, toasty almonds

DIRECTIONS

- In a big bowl, combine mayonnaise, vinegar, oil, poppy seeds, sugar, salt, and pepper.
- Toss in the spinach and strawberries after adding them.
- Sprinkle almonds on top.

Start your day off right with a kidney-friendly breakfast salad!

SALADS & SOUPS RECIPES

Cabbage - Onion - Sweet Pepper Medley

Cool and Crispy Cucumber

Strawberry Fruit Salad

Chicken & Fruit Salad

Broccoli-Bacon Salad

Green Curry Vegetable Soup

Chicken Chili with Sweet Potatoes

Spiralized Mediterranean Cucumber Salad

Sesame Tuna Salad

Cabbage-Onion -Sweet Pepper Medley

Nutrition Facts (Per Serving) Calories 70 Fat 4g Sodium 52g Carbs 8g Protein 1g Potassium 208 mg Phosphorus 29g

Prep time: 10 minutes Total time: 10 minutes Serving size 1 serving

Enjoy this colorful combination of red, green, and yellow peppers, onions, and cabbage to get your daily serving of vegetables. Ideal as a vegetarian dinner or side dish.

INGREDIENTS

1/2 cup of fresh red bell pepper •½ cup of fresh green bell peppers, •½ cup of fresh yellow bell pepper •½ cup of chopped fresh onions •2 cups shredded fresh cabbage •3 teaspoons of white vinegar •1 tablespoon of canola oil •1 1/2 tablespoons of brown sugar •1 1/2 teaspoons of Dijon mustard •1 1/2 teaspoons of pepper

DIRECTIONS

- •Bell peppers should be cut into thin, 2-inch pieces.
- Bell peppers, onion, and cabbage should be gently tossed together in a large nonstick pan.
- In a jar, combine the vinegar and the remaining ingredients.
- Tightly cover, and shake well.
- Stir gently as you add to the veggie mixture.
- Stirring regularly, saute the cabbage over medium heat until it is soft.

Cool and Crispy Cucumber

Nutrition Facts (Per Serving) Calories 27 Fat 2g Sodium 74g Carbs 3g Protein 0g Potassium 90 mg Phosphorus 14g

Prep time: 5 minutes Total time: 5 minutes Serving size 4 servings

Crisp, cool, and simple. Sliced cucumbers should be combined with fresh black pepper and sodium-free Italian dressing before being chilled and eaten.

INGREDIENTS

2 cups fresh cucumber, cut into 1/4-inch-thick rounds (peeling not necessary) •2 teaspoons of Italian or Caesar salad dressing •To taste, freshly ground black pepper

DIRECTIONS

- Combine the cucumber and salad dressing in a medium bowl with a cover.
- Shake to coat with the lid on.
- Add some freshly ground black pepper.
- Refrigerate.
- Ideally served cold.

Strawberry Fruit Salad

Nutrition Facts (Per Serving) Calories 70 Fat 0.6g Sodium 3g Carbs 17g Protein 1.4g Potassium 252 mg Phosphorus 38g

Prep time: 10 minutes Total time: 40 minutes Serving size 8 servings

This recipe for summer berry fruit salad yields plenty for a large gathering. Serve as a nutritious side dish at a potluck or at breakfast with granola and yogurt. The recipe can easily be altered to provide four servings.

INGREDIENTS

2 tablespoons of honey •2 tablespoons of lemon juice •6 cups fresh strawberries, hulled and cut in half (or quarters, if large) •2 cups of fresh blackberries •¼ cup of fresh mint, cut coarsely

DIRECTIONS

- In a big bowl, combine lemon juice and honey.
- Blackberries and strawberries should be added and gently mixed up.
- Let stand for 30 minutes to an hour at the very least.
- Just before serving, stir in the mint.

Chicken & Fruit Salad

Nutrition Facts (Per Serving)Calories 254 Fat 10.9g Sodium 322 g Carbs 18.4g Protein 20.6g Potassium 371 mg Phosphorus 171g

Prep time: 15 minutes Total time:15 minutes Serving size 6 cups greens, 2 cups each chicken & melon

A cool summer salad with chicken, melon, walnuts, and feta is topped with mixed salad greens. If you like, you may swap out the melon with your preferred summer fruit.

INGREDIENTS

1/4 cup low-fat sour cream •3 teaspoons of vinegar with a fruit flavor •4 teaspoons of sugar •1 1/2 tablespoons of Poppy seeds •4 teaspoons of salt •Freshly ground pepper, if desired •8 cups greens for a mixed salad •2 cups of cooked chicken breast, sliced •2 cups of melon, such cantaloupe or honeydew, cut •1/4 cup toasted, chopped walnuts •1/4 cup feta cheese crumbles

DIRECTIONS

- In a large bowl, stir together the sour cream, vinegar, sugar, poppy seeds, salt, and pepper.
- In a small dish, place 1/4 cup of the dressing aside.
- Toss the mixed greens with the dressing in the big basin.
- Chicken, melon, walnuts, and feta are added before being divided among four plates.
- 1 tablespoon of the leftover dressing should be drizzled over each serving.

Tip: To poach chicken breasts, put them in a medium skillet or saucepan with no bones and no skin.

Pour gently salted water over them, and then bring to a boil.

For 10 to 15 minutes, or when the chicken is well cooked and the center is no longer pink, cover the pot, lower the heat to low, and simmer the food gently. (Approximately 2 1/2 cups of cooked chicken is made from 1 pound of raw, boneless, skinless chicken breasts.)

Tip: To toast chopped nuts, add them to a small dry pan and let it simmer over medium-low heat, continually turning, until pleasant to the touch, 2 to 4 minutes.

Broccoli-Bacon Salad

Nutrition Facts (Per Serving) Calories 105 Fat 4.6g Sodium 160g Carbs 14.3g Protein 3.3g Potassium 233 mg Phosphorus 68g

Prep time: 20 minutes Total time: 20 minutes Serving size 6 serving, 1 scant cup each

This salad, a picnic classic, features broccoli, water chestnuts, cranberries, and a tiny bit of bacon. This variation is really creamy without being overly fatty.
Once you make it, you'll always have it on hand for your outdoor barbecues.

INGREDIENTS

1 minced garlic clove •1/4 cup of reduced-fat mayonnaise •1 8-ounce container of chopped and washed sliced water chestnuts •1/4 cup low-fat sour cream •2 teaspoons of cider vinegar •1/8 cup sugar •4 cups of broccoli crowns, cut finely •3 cooked bacon pieces, crumbled •3 tablespoons of cranberries, dried •Freshly ground pepper, if needed

DIRECTIONS

- In a large bowl, combine the garlic, mayonnaise, sour cream, vinegar, and sugar.

- Pepper, cranberries, bacon, broccoli, water chestnuts, and all of the above

- Stir to incorporate the dressing.

Green Curry Vegetable Soup

Nutrition Facts (Per Serving) Calories 243 Fat 4.6g Sodium 451g Carbs 39.3g Protein 15.9g Potassium 754 mg Phosphorus 282g

Prep time: 15 minutes Total time: 15 minutes Serving size 1 servings

Pour hot curry-flavored broth over noodles and vegetables in this very simple recipe for Thai noodle soup. You get a fast, filling soup while the veggies maintain their crispness. If you'd like to increase the amount of protein, feel free to add chicken, shrimp, or tofu.

INGREDIENTS

3/4 cup cooked whole-wheat angel hair pasta •1/2 cup fresh baby spinach •1/3 cup of chopped red bell pepper •1/4 cup carrots, grated •1/4 cup freshly chopped cilantro • 2 cups of chicken broth low in sodium • Thai green curry paste, 1 tablespoon, or more as desired

DIRECTIONS

- In a heatproof bowl, mix the spaghetti, spinach, bell pepper, carrot, and cilantro.
- Boil the chicken broth.
- Add the curry paste and stir.
- Over the pasta mixture, pour the broth.
- It's warm.

Chicken Chili with Sweet Potatoes

Nutrition Facts (Per Serving) Calories 324 Fat 9.8g Sodium 589g Carbs 34.9g Protein 26g Potassium 295 mg Phosphorus 793g

Prep time: 20 minutes Total time: 20 minutes Serving size 6 serving, 1 scant cup each

This nutritious one-pot chicken chili dish has a Southwestern twist because of the abundance of spices, maize, and bell pepper. Server with tortilla chips and your preferred spicy sauce. .

INGREDIENTS

2 tablespoons of extra virgin olive oil •1 big, chopped onion •3 minced garlic cloves •2 cups of half-inch-thick sweet potato cubes •1 chopped medium green bell pepper •2 tablespoons of chili powder •2 tablespoons of cumin powder •1 tsp. dried oregano •1 washed, 15-ounce can of low-sodium cannellini beans • 2 cups chicken broth (low sodium) or homemade chicken stock •1 cup of corn, frozen • 2 cups cooked chicken in half-inch cubes, or around 10 ounces • 3/4 cup of salt • 1/4 teaspoon of pepper, ground •As a garnish, use sour cream, avocado, and/or cilantro.

DIRECTIONS

- In a large saucepan, heat the oil to medium-high.
- Add the bell pepper, onion, sweet potato, and garlic; simmer, stirring occasionally, for 5 to 6 minutes, or until the veggies are just beginning to soften.
- Add the chili powder, cumin, and oregano, and stir-fry for 1 minute, or until flavorful.
- Bring to a boil the beans, broth, or stock.
- For 15 minutes, simmer gently over low heat with a half-cover.
- Stir in corn and raise heat to medium-high; cook for one minute.
- Cook the chicken for a further 1 to 2 minutes, or until thoroughly heated.
- Get rid of the heat. Add salt and pepper, and stir.
- If preferred, garnish the dish with sour cream, avocado, and/or cilantro.

Spiralized Mediterranean Cucumber Salad

Nutrition Facts (Per Serving) Calories 148 Fat 13.4g Sodium 290g Carbs 4.8g Protein 2.5g Potassium 169 mg Phosphorus 65g

Prep time: 20 minutes Total time: 20 minutes Serving size 6 servings

For this quick, time-saving vegetable side, spiralize crisp cucumber instead of slicing it. Wish to turn it into a meal? Simply add grilled chicken, shrimp, or chickpeas to a can.

INGREDIENTS

1/4 cup extra virgin olive oil •2 teaspoons red wine vinegar •1 tablespoon finely minced fresh oregano plus more for garnish •4 teaspoons of salt •1/4 teaspoon of pepper, ground •1-inch cucumber •1 cup cherry tomatoes, cut in half •1/2 cups of red onion, finely sliced •1/2 cup feta cheese in cubes •1/4 cup of sliced Kalamata olives

DIRECTIONS

- In a big bowl, combine oil, vinegar, oregano, salt, and pepper.
- Cut cucumbers lengthwise into "noodles" using a spiral vegetable slicer and the chipper blade attachment (for thick noodles).
- Noodles should be cut into 2-inch lengths.
- Toss the ingredients in the bowl with the dressing, including the cucumber noodles, tomatoes, onion, cheese, and olives.
- If preferred, top each serving with additional oregano.

Sesame Tuna Salad

Nutrition Facts (Per Serving) Calories 208 Fat 15.8g Sodium 383g Carbs 7.6g Protein 11.1g Potassium 422 mg Phosphorus 137g

Prep time: 25 minutes Total time: 25 minutes Serving size 2 cups tuna salad & 6 cups cabbage

A simple meal like canned tuna becomes a sophisticated meal when it is dipped in toasted sesame oil. If you happen to have romaine lettuce on hand, that would also work because we adore the crisp that napa cabbage adds to this salad.

INGREDIENTS

1/4 cup lemon juice or rice vinegar •3 tablespoons of canola oil •2 tablespoons of low-sodium soy sauce •1 teaspoon oil from toasted sesame •1½ teaspoons of sugar •1½ teaspoons of fresh ginger, minced •2 water-packed 5- to 6-ounce cans of chunk light tuna, drained •1 cup sliced snow peas or sugar snap peas •2 sliced scallions •6 cups of napa cabbage, thinly sliced •4 radishes, sliced or chopped into julienne •¼ cup of fresh leaves of cilantro •1 tablespoon of sesame seeds •Freshly ground pepper, to taste

DIRECTIONS

- In a small bowl, combine the ginger, sugar, canola oil, soy sauce, sesame oil, and vinegar (or lemon juice).
- Tuna, peas, and scallions are mixed with 3 tablespoons of the dressing in a medium bowl.
- Place the cabbage on 4 plates.
- Sprinkle radishes, cilantro, and sesame seeds on top of the middle of each plate where you placed one-fourth of the tuna mixture (approximately 1/2 cup).
- Sprinkle with pepper and drizzle with the remaining dressing (approximately 2 teaspoons per salad).

The secret to kidney health is a balanced diet unlock the secret with every meal!

APPETIZERS

Curried Cashews

Carrot Cake Energy Bites

Homemade Trail Mix

Heavenly Deviled Eggs Recipe

Tomato Phyllo Tart

Crispy Cauliflower Phyllo Cups Recipe

Cucumber & Tomato Salad with Preserved Lemon

Rustic Mushroom Tart

Curried Cashews

Nutrition Facts (Per Serving) Calories 101cal Fat 8g Sodium 163 g Carbs 6.2g Protein 2.7g Phosphorus 87g Potassium 107mg

Prep time: 5 minutes Total time: 50 minutes 6 cups (1 serving = 1/8 cup)

Every time we produced these curry cashews in the Kitchen, they were gone in a hurry due to their impossible addictive nature. Do not add salt if you are using salted cashews.

INGREDIENTS

6 teaspoons of Juice of lemons •6 tablespoons of Curry powder •4 tablespoons of kosher salt •6 cups of unsalted Cashews

DIRECTIONS

- Preheat the oven to 250°F and place racks in the top and bottom thirds.
- In a large bowl, combine salt, lemon juice, and curry powder.
- Add the cashews and stir to coat.
- Spread in an equal layer and divide between two big rimmed baking sheets.
- Bake for 45 minutes, stirring every 15 minutes, until dry.
- Allow it to fully cool.
- Keep in a tightly sealed container.

Carrot Cake Energy Bites

Nutrition Facts (Per Serving) Calories 48cal Fat 1.7g Sodium 31g Carbs 8.2g Protein 0.9g Potassium 87 mg Phosphorus 34g

Prep time: 15 minutes Total time: 15 minutes Serving size 22 bites (servings)

These no-cook energy snacks are simple to grab on the move and store nicely in the fridge or freezer.

INGREDIENTS

1 cup dates with pits •1/2 cup rolled old-fashioned oats •1/4 cup chopped pecans •1/4 cup of chia seeds •2 medium carrots, around 4 ounces, cut coarsely •1 teaspoon extract vanilla •1/4 teaspoon cinnamon powder •1/2 teaspoon of ginger, ground •1/4 teaspoon of powdered turmeric •1/4 teaspoon of salt •A pinch of ground pepper

DIRECTIONS

- In a food processor, mix the dates, oats, pecans, and chia seeds; pulse several times to blend and chop.
- When the paste starts to form, add the carrots, vanilla, cinnamon, ginger, turmeric, salt, and pepper. Process the ingredients until they are all finely minced.
- Using only 1 tablespoon per ball, form the mixture into balls.
- Serve.

Homemade Trail Mix

Nutrition Facts (Per Serving) Calories 149cal Fat 7. 4g Sodium 2g Carbs 20. 2g Protein 3.8g Potassium 278 mg Phosphorus 72g

Prep time: 15 minutes Total time: 15 minutes Serving size 22 bites (servings)

Any mix of nuts and dried fruits may be added to it.

INGREDIENTS

1/4 cup whole, unpeeled, shelled almonds •1/4 cup dry-roasted, unsalted peanuts •1/4 cup of dried cranberries •1/4 cup chopped dates with pits •2 ounces of dried fruit, such as apricots,

DIRECTIONS

- In a medium bowl, mix dates, apricots (or other fruit), cranberries, almonds, peanuts, and peanut butter.

Heavenly Deviled Eggs Recipe

Nutrition Facts (Per Serving) Calories 98cal Fat 7g Sodium 2g Carbs 2g Protein 6g Potassium 73mg Phosphorus 90g

Prep time: 10 minutes Total time: 10 minutes Serving size 4 servings (2 halves) Serves 4

This traditional and easy deviled egg dish is the way to go if you're looking for a fast, tasty snack that's usually a hit. Perfect whenever.

INGREDIENTS

Four big eggs, hard-boiled and shelled •2 teaspoons of light mayonnaise •1/2 tsp. dry mustard •1/2 tsp. of cider vinegar •1 tablespoon coarsely chopped onion •1/4 teaspoon of black pepper, ground •Dash of paprika as a garnish, if desired.

DIRECTIONS

- Eggs should be split lengthwise.
- Remove the yolks with care, then put them in a small basin.
- On a dish, place the egg white.
- Egg yolks are mashed with a fork, then mayonnaise, dry mustard, vinegar, onion, and freshly ground black pepper are added.
- Fill boiled egg whites slightly to the brim with the yolk mixture.
- Serve deviled eggs with paprika on top.

(**Optional**) Deviled eggs may be garnished with paprika before serving.\

Tomato Phyllo Tart

Nutrition Facts (Per Serving) Calories 144 cal Fat 9.1g Sodium 287 g Carbs 12.1g Protein 3.6g Potassium 112 mg Phosphorus 67g

Prep time: 30 minutes Total time: 1 hour 20 minutes Serving size 12 slices

Friends will be impressed by this vibrant tomato tart; no one needs to know how fast it come together. Basil completes the dish with a fragrant touch.

INGREDIENTS

•24 9-by-14-inch sheets of phyllo dough or 12 14-by-18-inch sheets •Extra virgin olive oil, 1/4 cup •1 teaspoon of simple, dry breadcrumbs •2 teaspoons of ready-made pesto •4 ounces or 3/4 cup of feta cheese crumbles •1 big red tomato, quarter-inch-thick slices •Slices of one big yellow tomato, 1/4-inch thick •1/2 kosher salt or to taste •Pepper, freshly ground, to taste •10–12 little basil leaves

DIRECTIONS

- Set the oven to 400°F. Using parchment paper, line a baking sheet measuring 17 1/2 by 12 1/2 inches. On the preheated pan, spread out one sizable piece of phyllo. (If using the smaller size, create a rectangle on the pan by gently overlapping two sheets.)
- The leftover phyllo should be kept protected with wax paper, plastic wrap, and a moist kitchen towel.
- Apply a thin layer of oil using a pastry brush on the phyllo surface.
- Add 1/4 teaspoon of breadcrumbs.
- Layer the remaining phyllo on top and repeat the previous procedure.
- The final sheet should be oil-brushed. To create the outside rim of the tart, carefully roll

- approximately 3/4 inch of each edge toward the center.

- Apply pesto evenly over the earth's surface using the same brush.

- Over the pesto layer, scatter approximately half of the crumbled feta cheese.

- Salt and pepper the tomato slices as you alternate their colors over the pesto layer. The remaining cheese should then he added on top.

- Bake for 30 to 35 minutes, or until the crust is golden and crispy.

- Allow the pan to cool on a wire rack for five minutes.

- Lift the parchment paper to serve, then put the tart onto a large dish or cutting board.

- Add basil leaves to the surface.

- At room temperature or heated, serve.

Crispy Cauliflower Phyllo Cups Recipe

Nutrition Facts (Per Serving) Calories 68 cal Fat 5g Sodium 107g Carbs 2g Protein 3g Potassium 42 mg Phosphorus 49g

Prep time: 30 minutes Total time: 45 minutes Serving size 1 serving Makes 24 cups

Scrambled eggs, bacon, cauliflower, cheese, and jalapenos are added to flaky, light phyllo pastry cups before being baked to a golden brown perfection. Ideal for any party spread or breakfast.

INGREDIENTS

3 beaten eggs with a gentle scrambling •1/2 cup of low-sodium shredded Swiss cheese •12 cup shredded cheddar cheese •2 tablespoons of butter •4 chopped slices of natural, uncured bacon •1 1/2 cups chopped, cooked, and thoroughly drained cauliflower •1/4 cup finely diced onions •2 teaspoons diced jalapenos •1/2 tsp. red pepper flakes •A teaspoon of parsley •1/2 teaspoon of black pepper, ground •3 phyllo dough sheets

Optional: Black pepper and parsley as garnishes.

DIRECTIONS

- Preheat the oven to 375° F.
- Eggs should be softly scrambled in a large sauté pan before being taken out and placed aside.
- Melt the butter in the same pan.
- Cook the bacon in a skillet.
- Once the onions are transparent, add the cauliflower, jalapenos, and red pepper flakes.
- Add ground black pepper and parsley for flavor.
- Add scrambled eggs and two cheeses after removing them from the heat.
- Phyllo sheets are in layer three.

- Cut sheets into 24 squares, then press them into a small muffin tray that has been gently sprayed.

- Equal portions of the mixture should be placed in each muffin cup.

- Bake on the lowest rack of the oven for 12 to 15 minutes, or until the sides are just beginning to turn brown.

- Switch off the oven, then wait two to three minutes.

Cucumber & Tomato Salad with Preserved Lemon

Nutrition Facts (Per Serving) Calories 91 cal Fat 7.2g Sodium 127 g Carbs 6.4g Protein 1.2g Potassium 275mg Phosphorus 275g

Prep time: 25 minutes Total time: 35 minutes Serving size 4

Preserved lemon gives this cucumber and tomato salad a tart, salty bite. If you'd like, lemon zest might work well in place of this. Serve this nutritious salad as a side dish over a bed of finely julienned purple kale that has been gently seasoned with more olive oil and lemon juice, or as a complement to foods like grilled lamb or chicken.

INGREDIENTS

3 cups tiny, chopped, unpeeled cucumbers—preferably Persian or "mini" •1 1/2 cups halved or quartered various cherry tomatoes •1/4 cup of white onion, coarsely chopped •3 tablespoons of fresh parsley, roughly chopped •1 tablespoon of fresh mint, roughly chopped •1 teaspoon of lemon zest or 2 tablespoons of minced preserved lemon •1 tablespoon of lemon juice, fresh •1/4 teaspoon of kosher salt •2 teaspoons of extra virgin olive oil •Freshly ground pepper, if desired

DIRECTIONS

- In a medium bowl, mix the preserved lemon (or zest), lemon juice, salt, cucumbers, tomatoes, onions, parsley, and mint.
- For the flavors to combine, let stand for at least 10 minutes (and as long as 2 hours).
- Add oil and coat by tossing. Use pepper to season.
- Serve immediately.

Tips

Advice: Persian cucumbers are almost seedless and have skin that is thin enough to be eaten raw.

They are interchangeable with the similar but bigger English cucumber and are typically 5 to 6 inches long.

Plan ahead: Allow to stand for up to two hours at room temperature.

Rustic Mushroom Tart

Nutrition Facts (Per Serving) Calories 155 cal Fat 9g Sodium 230g Carbs 12.7g Protein 4.9g Potassium 129 mg Phosphorus 80g

Prep time: 30 minutes Total time: 1 hour Serving size 12 slices

Don't allow the reputation of phyllo dough as being difficult to build to deter you; this pie is really fairly easy to put together and keeps you eating healthily thanks to our way of drizzling olive oil and scattering breadcrumbs between the layers. It may be eaten as an appetizer or as a main meal if it is sliced into smaller pieces.

INGREDIENTS

Ricotta cheese, part-skim, 3/4 cup •2 ounces of soft goat cheese in a half-cup •2 tablespoons freshly chopped rosemary •pepper, freshly ground,   to taste •1 teaspoon of butter •4 cups of chopped wild mushrooms, mixed •1 big leek, just the white portion,   cut in half lengthwise, sliced thinly, and rinsed well •Salt,   1/2 teaspoons •White wine,   1/4 cup •Thawed phyllo dough on 10 sheets (14 by 18 inches) or 20 sheets (9 by 14 inches) •Extra virgin olive oil, 1/4 cup •1/4 cup of simple, dry breadcrumbs

DIRECTIONS

- In a medium bowl, mix the ricotta, goat cheese, rosemary, and pepper. Place aside.
- In a large skillet,   set over medium-high heat, melt the butter.
- Cook,   stirring,   the mushrooms, leek, and salt until the leek begins to soften and the mushrooms start to release their juices, approximately 3 minutes.
- Wine should be added and simmered for approximately two minutes, or until the liquid has evaporated. Place aside.
- Set the oven to 400°F.

- Use parchment paper to line a large baking sheet (12 by 17 inches, roughly). On the preheated pan, spread out one sizable piece of phyllo. (If utilizing the smaller size, create a rectangle by gently overlapping two pages.)

- The leftover phyllo should be kept protected with wax paper, plastic wrap, and a moist kitchen towel.

- With a pastry brush, lightly grease the phyllo. Add a teaspoon of breadcrumbs. Layer the remaining phyllo on top and repeat the previous procedure.

- To create the outside rim of the tart, carefully roll approximately 3/4 inch of each edge toward the center.

- Over the phyllo, evenly distribute the reserved cheese mixture. Add the saved mushroom mixture on top.

- Bake for 25 to 30 minutes, or until the crust is golden and crisp.

- Allow the pan to cool on a wire rack for five minutes. Lift the parchment paper to serve, then put the tart onto a large dish or cutting board.

- It's hot.

- Before making the dish, thaw the frozen phyllo (in its packaging) at room temperature for two hours or in the refrigerator for at least eight hours or overnight.

Top off your meal with a kidney-friendly dessert!

DESSERTS

Caramel Apples

Chocolate Coconut Macaroons

Chocolate Nut Bark

Flourless Chocolate Cookies

Mini Pecan Pies

Pineapple Nice Cream

Watermelon Fruit Pizza

Indoor S'more

Lemon Curd

Blueberry Corn Cobbler

Caramel Apples

Nutrition Facts (Per Serving) Calories 228cal Fat 6.4g Sodium 55g Carbs 44.1g Protein 1.6g Potassium 206 mg Phosphorus 35g

Prep time: 15 minutes Total time: 45 minutes Serving size 6 caramel apples

Just enough caramel is used in this delectable dessert to give each pic of food a pleasant touch of salty-sweet taste.

INGREDIENTS

1/3 cup of light brown sugar in bags •1/4 ounces of agave nectar •2 tablespoons of butter •1/8 teaspoon salt •3 tablespoons of chopped, unsalted nuts, such as pecans or peanuts •6 little apples, like Eve or Paula Red

DIRECTIONS

- Cooking spray should be used after placing wax paper on a baking pan.
- Apply cooking spray to a tablespoon-size measuring device.
- In a small saucepan, combine butter, brown sugar, agave, and salt.
- Place over medium heat; once the syrup begins to faintly bubble around the edge, simmer for an additional minute while continually stirring.
- Cook the nuts with the sugar, stirring frequently, for approximately a minute, until the sugar has melted and the mixture has darkened.
- Get rid of the heat.
- Spork each with roughly 1 spoonful of caramel, rapidly.

- Repeat the process, rotating each apple as you pour another spoonful of caramel over it.

- Allow the baking sheet to cool for five minutes. Place craft or popsicle sticks within the tops.

- Reapply any stray caramel strands to the apples.

- Give it at most 30 minutes to cool.

Tips

Making ahead: For up to a day, keep in wax paper at room temperature.

Wooden popsicle/craft sticks as equipment

Chocolate Coconut Macaroons

Nutrition Facts (Per Serving) Calories 89cal Fat 6.3g Sodium 16g Carbs 8.1g Protein 1g Potassium 63mg Phosphorus 22g

Prep time: 25 minutes Total time: 40 minutes Serving size 20 macaroons

This recipe for a healthy dessert upgrades light coconut biscuits with a drizzle of dark chocolate.

INGREDIENTS

2 big egg whites •1/2 cup sugar •2 1/4 cups of unsweetened coconut shredded •1 teaspoon of almond or vanilla essence •A dash of salt •1 ounce of chopped and melted dark chocolate

DIRECTIONS

- Set the oven to 350°F.
- Use parchment paper to line a big baking sheet with a rim.
- Using an electric mixer, beat the egg whites in a medium basin until soft peaks form.
- Beat the meringue while adding sugar until glossy. Add salt, vanilla (or almond) extract, and coconut to the mixture.
- 20 balls made from the mixture, each using approximately 1 tablespoon, should be placed on the baking sheet that has been prepared.
- The macaroons should be baked for 15 to 20 minutes, or until the outsides are gently browned but the inside are still soft.
- To cool, transfer to a wire rack.

- Put the chocolate in a little plastic bag. Cut a very little corner off.

- Pour the chocolate over the cooled cookies after forcing it through the hole. Alternately, swiftly wave a fork dipped in chocolate over the cookies.

- Before serve for storing the cookies, let them stand until the chocolate hardens.

Chocolate Nut Bark

Nutrition Facts (Per Serving) Calories 74cal Fat 5.4g Sodium 1g Carbs 7.2g Protein 1.2g Potassium 67mg Phosphorus 33g

Prep time: 10 minutes Total time: 35 minutes

This fast and simple chocolate nut bark may be made using your favorite nuts.

INGREDIENTS

2 cups of melted milk, bittersweet, or semisweet chocolate chips •1 1/2 cups of different nuts, including cashews, almonds, and hazelnuts, plus more for garnish

DIRECTIONS

- Use foil to cover the baking sheet with a rim. (Be careful to prevent wrinkling.)
- In a larger dish, mix the melted chocolate and the nuts. Spread the ingredients into a 12-by-9-inch rectangle on the foil using a spatula.
- If preferred, add more finely chopped nuts. 20 minutes or so in the refrigerator will get it set.
- On a cutting board, transfer the bark and foil.
- Slice into 1 1/2-inch pieces with a sharp knife.

Flourless Chocolate Cookies

Nutrition Facts (Per Serving) Calories 74cal Fat 2.5g Sodium 27g Carbs 12.6g Protein 1.1g Potassium 68mg Phosphorus 26g

Prep time: 15 minutes Total time: 20 minutes Serving size 16 cookies

These gluten-free, melt-in-your-mouth cookies are made without flour and receive their volume from beaten egg whites, much like meringue. Each mouthful has a chocolate chip to enhance the taste of the luscious chocolate.

INGREDIENTS

1 cup of confectioners' sugar •1/4 cup bittersweet cocoa powder •1/8 teaspoon salt •2 big egg whites •Vanilla extract, 1 teaspoon •1/2 cup chopped bittersweet chocolate chunks or chips

DIRECTIONS

- Set the oven to 350°F. Two big baking sheets should be lined with parchment paper.
- Drizzle some cooking spray on the paper.
- In a medium bowl, mix salt, cocoa, and confectioners' sugar.
- Egg whites are beaten with an electric mixer in a large mixing basin until soft peaks form.
- Include vanilla. Utilizing a rubber spatula, integrate the cocoa mixture into the batter. Add chocolate chunks or chips and combine.
- Using a tablespoon, drop the batter onto the prepared baking sheets,

spacing each cookie approximately two inches apart.

- Take the cookies for 12 to 14 minutes, one sheet at a time, or until the tops are just starting to crack.

- Before transferring to a wire rack to finish cooling down, let the food cool slightly on the pan.

Tips for planning ahead: For up to three days, keep cookies in an airtight container.

Mini Pecan Pies

Nutrition Facts (Per Serving) Calories 124 cal Fat 7.6g Sodium 105g Carbs 12.8g Protein 1.9g Potassium 58mg Phosphorus 45mg

Prep time: 40 minutes Total time: 55 minutes Serving size 24 mini pies

The secret to these luscious delights is portion control; by baking them in mini-muffin pans, you can control the amount of carbohydrates and saturated fat they contain. Additionally, you may prepare this pecan pie recipe without corn syrup by using maple syrup.

INGREDIENTS

1 1/2 cups rolled old-fashioned oats •1/2 cup all-purpose flour •1/2 cup split-packed light brown sugar •1 salty teaspoon, divide •1 stick of cold, unsalted butter with 8 tablespoons, broken up into tiny pics •2 huge eggs •4 ounces of pure maple syrup •1 cup of toasted and coarsely sliced pecan halves •Vanilla extract, 1 teaspoon

DIRECTIONS

- Set the oven to 350°F. Apply cooking spray to 24 mini-muffin cups.
- In a food processor, combine oats, flour, 1/4 cup brown sugar, and 1/2 teaspoon salt.
- Process the oats until they are powdery.
- Spread out the butter pieces on top and process just long enough for a dough to form.
- Using about 1 1/2 tablespoons of dough per mini-muffin cup, divide the dough among the prepared cups.

- Each cup should have dough pressed into the bottom and up the sides.
- The crusts should bake for approximately 15 minutes, or until the edge are brown and firm.
- The crusts will have slightly blown up while baking; use the back of a spoon to push them back down and up the edge.
- In a larger dish, combine the eggs, remaining 1/4 cup brown sugar, 1/2 teaspoon salt, maple syrup, pecans, and vanilla.
- Use around 1/2 spoonful of filling for each crust as you divide the mixture among them.
- Bake small pies for 10 to 12 minutes, or until the filling is set. Allow the pan to cool for at least 15 minutes.
- Release the edge with an offset spatula, then move to a wire rack to finish cooling.

Tips:

Equipment: 24 cup mini-muffin tin

Pineapple Nice Cream

Nutrition Facts (Per Serving) Calories 55 cal Fat 0.2g Sodium 1mg Carbs 14.2g Protein 0.6g Potassium 131 mg Phosphorus 10g

Prep time: 5 minutes Total time: 5 minutes Serving size 3 cups

The characteristics of "nice cream, " a healthy substitute for ice cream, include being entirely fruit-based, being dairy-free, and having no added sugar. Tropical tastes are present in this lovely pineapple cream, owing to the addition of mango and lime. This naturally sweet frozen treat may be made in a food processor or blender in a matter of minutes. Enjoy it by itself or with toasted coconut and fresh fruit on top.

INGREDIENTS

1 box (16 ounces) of frozen pineapple chunks •1 big mango, peeled, seeded, and diced, or 1 cup frozen mango pics •1 teaspoon of lime or lemon juice

DIRECTIONS

- In a food processor, blend pineapple, mango, and lemon (or lime) juice until they are smooth and creamy. (You may need to add up to 1/4 cup water if you're using frozen mango.)
- Serve immediately for the finest texture.

Watermelon Fruit Pizza

Nutrition Facts (Per Serving) Calories 144 cal Fat 9.1g Sodium 287 g Carbs 12.1g Protein 3.6g Potassium 112 mg Phosphorus 67g

Prep time: 10 minutes Total time: 10 minutes Serving size 8 servings

This recipe for fruit dessert pizza replaces the traditional cookie crust with a healthier watermelon crust. " This fresh dessert, which is topped with yogurt sauce, your preferred berries, and mint, may easily be duplicated for a party or cut in half for daily use.

INGREDIENTS

1/2 cup plain, low-fat yogurt •1 tsp. of honey •Vanilla extract, 1/4 teaspoon •2 substantial spherical slices of watermelon, cut from the melon's middle and approximately an inch thick •2/3 cup of sliced strawberries •Half a cup of blackberries •2 teaspoons of freshly torn mint

DIRECTIONS

- In a small dish, mix the yogurt, honey, and vanilla.
- Each slice of watermelon should have 1/4 cup of the yogurt mixture on it.
- Create 8 wedges out of each slice.
- Add strawberries, blackberries, and mint to the top.

Indoor S'more

Nutrition Facts (Per Serving) Calories 103 cal Fat 3.6g Sodium 44 mg Carbs 17g Protein 1.1g Potassium 62 mg Phosphorus 33 mg

Prep time: 5 minutes Total time: 5 minutes Serving size 4 servings

S'mores may be enjoyed without being in close proximity to a fire. Just make sure to keep an eye on them under the broiler since marshmallows may quickly go from nicely toasted to charcoal.

INGREDIENTS

2 Graham crackers whole, cut in half •Four marshmallows •2 teaspoons of melted bittersweet chocolate chips

DIRECTIONS

- Heat the broiler while positioning the oven rack in the top third of the oven.
- On a baking sheet, arrange the graham cracker halves. Place 1 marshmallow on each.
- With the oven door slightly ajar and careful observation, broil the marshmallows for 45 to 75 seconds, or until they are golden brown.
- After removing them from the oven, add a little melted chocolate to each s'more.

Tip:

Microwave chocolate for one minute on medium to melt it. Stir, then microwave on medium for a further 20 seconds at a time until melted. Alternately, put the chocolate on the top of a double boiler over warm water that is not boiling. until melted, stir

Lemon Curd

Nutrition Facts (Per Serving) Calories 150.7cal Fat 10.7g Sodium 44 mg Carbs 9.5g Protein 4.3g Potassium 57.93mg Phosphorus 75.21mg

Prep time: 5 minutes Total time: 10-15 minutes Serving size 8 servings

INGREDIENTS

5-egg yolks •2 tablespoons fresh lemon zest •1/2 cup of lemon juice •Confectioners' sugar, half a cup •1-tablespoon vanilla extract •1/4 cup of margarine

DIRECTIONS

- A medium saucepan should be just partially filled with water and heated to a simmer.
- Add the egg yolks, sugar, lemon juice, lemon zest, and vanilla to a medium heat-resistant bowl.
- Mix thoroughly, then set aside for two minutes.
- Put the bowl over the burner and gradually heat it while whisking for 7-8 minutes, or until it thickens.
- Margarine should be added after the mixture has been removed from the heat and mixed well.
- Cool in the refrigerator.
- Take pleasure in pies and scones!

Blueberry Corn Cobbler

Nutrition Facts (Per Serving) Calories 216 cal Fat 2g Sodium 48.3mg Carbs 45.5g Protein 2.9g Potassium 153.89mg Phosphorus 63.09mg

Prep time: 15 minutes Total time: 35 minutes Serving size 1/9th of a 9-inch square pan

INGREDIENTS

1/3 cup (79 ml) of milk •1 egg •2 tablespoons (30 g) unsalted butter •2. 5 g of cream of tartar in 1/2 tsp. •1. 25 g of 1/4 tsp. baking soda •1 1/4 cups (156 grams) of white corn flour •170 ml or 3/4 cups of honey •806 g (4 cups) of blueberries

DIRECTIONS

- Preheat the oven to 375°F.
- In a mixing basin, combine the milk, egg, butter, cream of tartar, and baking soda.
- Stir thoroughly to remove any lumps before adding the corn flour and 1/2 cup of honey.
- In a 9-inch baking dish, spread the berries evenly.
- Over the berries, drizzle the rest of the honey.
- By tablespoons, sprinkle the batter over the berries.
- Bake for 30 to 35 minutes, or until the crust is golden brown and the berries are bubbling.

Your Renal Diet Snacks are your partners in health - make them a priority

SNACKS

Sesame Carrots

Cucumber Bites

Peanut Butter Oats Energy Balls

Orange & Cinnamon Biscotti

Sweet Cornbread Muffins With Citrus Honey Butter

Roasted Pumpkin Seeds

Bev's Chocolate Chip Cookies

Gorp

Roasted Garlic and Ricotta Crostini

Sesame Carrots

Nutrition Facts (Per Serving) Calories 50 cal Fat 1. 6g Sodium 72mg Carbs 8.4g Protein 1.1g Potassium 232 mg Phosphorus 45g

Prep time: 5 minutes Total time: 5 minutes Serving size 2 cups (⅔ cup per serving)

On a platter of carrots, toasted sesame seeds provide flavor and visual appeal.

INGREDIENTS

Baby carrots, 2 cups •Sesame seeds, roasted, in a tablespoon •A pinch of dried thyme •A pinch of kosher salt

DIRECTIONS

- In a small bowl, toss carrots with sesame seeds, thyme, and kosher salt.
- Serve

Cucumber Bites

Nutrition Facts (Per Serving) Calories 120 cal Fat 7.8g Sodium 212 mg Carbs 7.5g Protein 6.2g Potassium 186 mg Phosphorus 136g

Prep time: 5 minutes Total time: 5 minutes Serving size 6 cucumber bites

Cucumbers are topped in this fast, gluten-free snack dish with hummus, cheese, and a dash of spicy sauce.

INGREDIENTS

6 slices of cucumber •2 tablespoons of hummus, plain •2 tablespoons of Cheddar cheese, shredded •Squeeze of Sriracha spicy sauce

DIRECTIONS

- Each cucumber slice should have a thin layer of hummus on top, followed by cheese.
- Add a few sriracha dots to the top of each slice.

Peanut Butter Oats Energy Balls

Nutrition Facts (Per Serving) Calories 71 cal Fat 3g Sodium 23 mg Carbs 10.4g Protein 1.8g Potassium 102 mg Phosphorus 37g

Prep time: 15 minutes Total time: 30 minutes Serving size 12 servings

These no-bake energy balls are held together by sweet, sticky dates. This snack travels easily and is ideal for hiking or sports.
Use Medjool dates, the biggest and most delicious date kind, for the finest taste and texture.
Find them with other dried fruits or in the produce section.

INGREDIENTS

3/4 cup chopped Medjool dates •1/2 cup of rolled oats •1/4 cup of Natural peanut butter •Chia seeds as an ornament

DIRECTIONS

- Dates should be soaked for 5 to 10 minutes in a small dish of boiling water. Then drain.
- Process the soaking dates, oats, and peanut butter until they are very finely ground in a food processor.
- Form into 12 balls, each about a tablespoon in size.
- If preferred, add chia seeds as a garnish.
- Place in the refrigerator for up to a week, or at least 15 minutes.

Tip: Because oats are often contaminated with what and barley, those who have celiac disease or gluten sensitivity should only consume oats that are marked "gluten-free. "

Orange & Cinnamon Biscotti

Nutrition Facts (Per Serving) Calories 144 cal Fat 9.1g Sodium 287 g Carbs 12.1g Protein 3.6g Potassium 112 mg Phosphorus 67g

Prep time: 30 minutes Total time: 1 hour 35 minutes Serving size 18 cookies (1 serving =1 cookie)

Enjoy the zesty flavor of orange, warmed with a dash of cinnamon, and presented in a crunchy biscotti. Dip in coffee or tea, or serve as a dessert or snack.

INGREDIENTS

1 cup of sugar •1/2 cup room-temperature unsalted butter •2 big eggs •2 tablespoons orange peel, grated •1 teaspoon vanilla extract •2 cups all-purpose flour •1 teaspoon tartar sauce •1/2 teaspoon baking soda •1 teaspoon cinnamon powder •1/4 teaspoon of salt

DIRECTIONS

- Nonstick cooking spray should be sprayed on two baking sheets.
- In a large mixing basin, combine the sugar and unsalted butter.
- Add the eggs one at a time, carefully beating after each addition.
- Mix in the orange peel and vanilla extract.
- In a medium-sized mixing bowl, combine the flour, cream of tartar, baking soda, cinnamon, and salt.
- Mix the dry ingredients into the butter mixture until they are well combined.
- Cut the dough in half. Position half on the prepared baking sheet. Form each half into a 3-inch-wide by

3-quarter-inch-high log shape with lightly floured hands.

- Bake for 35 minutes, or until the dough logs are firm to the touch.
- Remove the dough logs from the oven and set the aside for 10 minutes to cool.
- Move logs to the work surface. Using a serrated knife, cut 12-inch-thick pieces on the diagonal.
- Place on baking pans, cut side down.
- Bake for 12 minutes, or until the bottoms are brown.
- Bake until the bottoms of the biscotti are brown, about 12 minutes more.
- Before serving, cool on a wire rack.

TIP: Refrigerate the dough for thirty minutes before shaping it into logs.

Sweet Cornbread Muffins With Citrus Honey Butter

Nutrition Facts (Per Serving) Calories 208 cal Fat 13g Sodium 179 mg Carbs 20g Protein 3g Potassium 87 mg Phosphorus 67g

Prep time: 20 minutes Total time: 40 minutes Serving size 1 serving (1 muffin)

These are the best muffins in the world! They provide an excellent accompaniment to a main meal, soup, or salad. They're nearly dessert when served with citrus honey butter! Sweet.

INGREDIENTS

1 pound cornmeal •1 cup of flour •1 1/2 tablespoon baking soda •3 tablespoons of lemon juice •1 been egg •1 cup of milk •1/2 pound unsalted butter, melted •1 tablespoon of vanilla extract

Honey and butter:

2 teaspoons honey •1 pound softened unsalted butter •1/2 tsp orange zest •1/4 tsp black pepper •1/2 teaspoon orange extract

DIRECTIONS

- Preheat the oven to 400°F.
- In a large mixing basin, combine the egg, milk, and butter until thoroughly combined.
- Separate the flour, cornmeal, and baking soda, then stir into the liquid ingredients until smooth. Make sure not to overestimate.
- Fill each muffin cup 34 full with muffin liners and bake for 15-20 minutes on the center rack.
- In a small bowl, mix together the honey and butter ingredients until smooth; spread on top of cornbread muffins or serve on the side.

TIP: Make tiny muffins and serve alongside soup or salad.

Roasted Pumpkin Seeds

Nutrition Facts (Per Serving) Calories 54 cal Fat 2.8g Sodium 50mg Carbs 5.7g Protein 2g Potassium 98 mg Phosphorus 10g

Prep time:15 minutes Total time: 35 minutes Serving size 1 cup for 6 servings

Save the pumpkin seeds from your Halloween pumpkin so you can make this crunchy, healthful snack.

INGREDIENTS

1 cup freshly ground pumpkin seeds •1 tsp. canola oil •1/8 teaspoon of salt

DIRECTIONS

- Preheat the oven to 350°F with the rack in the center.
- Use parchment paper or a non-stick baking mat to line a rimmed baking sheet.
- Drizzle oil over pumpkin seeds in a small dish and swirl to coat.
- Stir in the salt and coat well. Spread in an equal layer on the prepared baking sheet.
- Bake for 20 minutes, stirring once or twice, until toasted and golden brown.
- Using paper towels, pat dry.

Tips

Scoop out the interior of the pumpkin to extract the seeds. Separate the seeds as best you can from the flesh, then set them in a dish of water. Swish the seeds around with your palms to dislodge any residual flesh or threads.

The seeds will float to the surface and may be removed with a spoon or your fingertips. Pat dry with paper towels after draining the seeds on a dry dish towel or a plate lined with paper towels.

For up to 3 days, keep in an airtight container.

Bev's Chocolate Chip Cookies

Nutrition Facts (Per Serving) Calories 99cal Fat 5.5g Sodium 64 mg Carbs 12.5g Protein 1.3g Potassium 49 mg Phosphorus 34g

Prep time: 10 minutes Total time: 35 minutes Serving size about 2 1/2 dozen cookies

INGREDIENTS

3/4 cup rolled oats •1 cup whole-grain flour •1/2 teaspoon baking soda •1/2 teaspoon of salt •1/4 cup softened butter •1/4 cup of canola oil •1/3 cup of granulated sugar •1/3 cup of brown sugar •1 big egg •A teaspoon of vanilla extract •1 cup of chocolate chips

DIRECTIONS

- Preheat the oven to 350°F. Apply nonstick cooking spray to two baking sheets.

- The oats should be crushed in a food processor or blender. In a medium mixing basin, whisk together the flour, baking soda, and salt.

- In a large mixing basin, cream butter with an electric mixer until creamy.

- Mix in the oil, granulated sugar, brown sugar, egg, and vanilla extract until the mixture is smooth and creamy.

- While the mixer is running, add the dry ingredients and mix on low until barely blended. Mix in the chocolate chips.

- Drop the dough by heaping teaspoonful onto the prepared baking sheets, at least 1 inch apart.

- Take the cookies, one sheet at a time, for approximately 15 minutes, or until firm around the edge and golden on top.

- Cool the cookies on the baking pans for 2 minutes before transferring them to wire racks to cool fully.

Tip: Store the cookies in an airtight jar for up to 3 days or freeze for up to 2 months.

Gorp

Nutrition Facts (Per Serving) Calories 99cal Fat 6.3g Sodium 16mg Carbs 10.1g Protein 2.6g Potassium 111 mg Phosphorus 54g

Prep time: 5 minutes Total time: 5 minutes Serving size 2 servings

Description
Try adding your favorite dried fruits and nuts to this simple recipe.

INGREDIENTS
1/2 ounces whole shelled (unpeeled) almonds •1/4 ounces dry-roasted unsalted peanuts •1/4 ounce dried cranberries •1 tablespoon pitted, chopped dates •1 1/2 tsp. chocolate chips

DIRECTIONS
- In a small mixing bowl, combine almonds, peanuts, cranberries, dates, and chocolate chips.

Roasted Garlic and Ricotta Crostini

Nutrition Facts (Per Serving) Calories 136.5cal Fat 3.8g Sodium 212 mg Carbs 20g Protein 5.8g Potassium 97 mg Phosphorus 80g

Prep time: 5 minutes Total time: 5 minutes Servings per recipe: 6 Serving size: 1 slice

INGREDIENTS

6 pieces of baguette •2 tablespoons of fresh herbs •2 roasted garlic cloves •a little black pepper •1/2 cup ricotta cheese

DIRECTIONS

- Combine the ricotta, herbs, and roasted garlic in a mixing bowl.
- Spread on pieces of baguette, then broil until crusty.
- Enjoy while serving!

Eat with a fresh greens such as this ***Pear and Arugula Salad***

Sip your way to a better health with delicious, nutritious Renal Diet Smoothies

SMOOTHIES

Easy Pineapple Protein Smoothie

Fruity Smoothie

Mixed Berry Protein Smoothie

Peach High-Protein Fruit Smoothie

Strawberry High-Protein Fruit Smoothie

Banana-Apple Smoothie

Berry Smoothie

Spicy Pina Colada Smoothie

Peach Raspberry Smoothie

Easy Pineapple Protein Smoothie

Nutrition Facts (Per Serving) Calories 268 cal Fat 4g Sodium 93 mg Carbs 40g Protein 18g Potassium 237 mg Phosphorus 160g

Prep time: 5 minutes Total time: 5 minutes Serving size 10 ounces per serving

INGREDIENTS

3/4 cup sherbet or sorbet pineapple •1 sprinkling vanilla whey protein powder •1 cup of water

Optional: 2 ice cubes

DIRECTIONS

- Blend pineapple sherbet, whey protein powder, and water in a blender (ice cubes are optional).
- Blend for 30 to 45 seconds right away.

Fruity Smoothie

Nutrition Facts (Per Serving) Calories 186 cal Fat 2g Sodium 62 mg Carbs 2g Protein 23g Potassium 282 mg Phosphorus 118g

Prep time: 5 minutes Total time: 5 minutes Serving size 2 servings (1- ½ cups)

INGREDIENTS

8 ounces canned fruit cocktail mixed with juice •2 scoops whey protein powder with vanilla flavor •1 cup ice water •1 cup of crushed ice

DIRECTIONS

- In a blender, combine all of the ingredients.
- Divide into two equal portions and serve.

Mixed Berry Protein Smoothie

Nutrition Facts (Per Serving) Calories 152 cal Fat 4g Sodium 84 mg Carbs 15g Protein 14g Potassium 216 mg Phosphorus 76g

Prep time: 5 minutes Total time: 5 minutes Serving size 2 servings (7 ounces)

INGREDIENTS

4 ounces of extremely cold water •1 cup mixed berries, fresh or frozen •2 cubes of ice •1 teaspoon liquid flavor enhancer droplets Crystal Light®, any berry flavor •1 pound whipped cream topping •2 tablespoons whey protein powder

DIRECTIONS

- Blend together water, frozen berries, ice cubes, and liquid flavor enhancer drops in a blender.
- Blend till slushy and thoroughly combined.
- Blend in the whipped topping.
- Mix in the protein powder.
- Blend well.
- Divide into two portions and serve one immediately, or freeze and thaw for later.

Peach High-Protein Fruit Smoothie

Nutrition Facts (Per Serving) Calories 132 cal Fat 0g Sodium 154 mg Carbs 24g Protein 10g Potassium 353 mg Phosphorus 36g

Prep time: 5 minutes Total time: 5 minutes Serving size 1 serving

INGREDIENTS

1/2 cup of ice •2 tbsp. powdered egg whites •3/4 cup of fresh peaches •1 tablespoon of sugar

DIRECTIONS

- In a blender, puree the peaches until smooth.
- Blend in all of the remaining ingredients until smooth.
- Serve right away

Strawberry High-Protein Fruit Smoothie

Nutrition Facts (Per Serving) Calories 156cal Fat 0g Sodium 215mg Carbs 25g Protein 14g Potassium 400mg Phosphorus 49g

Prep time: 5 minutes Total time: 5 minutes Serving size 1 serving

INGREDIENTS

3/4 cup freshly picked strawberries •1/2 cup pasteurized liquid egg whites •1/2 cup of ice •1 teaspoon sugar

DIRECTIONS

- Blend strawberries till smooth in a blender.
- Blend in all of the remaining ingredients until smooth.
- Serve right away.

Banana-Apple Smoothie

Nutrition Facts (Per Serving) Calories 292 cal Fat 0g Sodium 103 mg Carbs 61g Protein 9g Potassium 609 mg Phosphorus 140g

Prep time: 5 minutes Total time: 5 minutes Serving size 1 cup

INGREDIENTS

1/2 banana, peeled and sliced •1/2 cup unsweetened yogurt •1/2 cup unsweetened applesauce •1/4 cup almond milk or rice milk •1 teaspoon honey •2 tbsp. oat or wheat bran

DIRECTIONS

- In a blender, combine the banana, yogurt, applesauce, milk, and honey.
- Blend until completely smooth.
- Blend in the oat bran until it is thickened.

Berry Smoothie

Nutrition Facts (Per Serving) Calories 188 cal Fat 3g Sodium 6 mg Carbs 28g Protein 8g Potassium 163 mg Phosphorus 30g

Prep time: 5 minutes Total time: 5 minutes Serving size 1 cup

INGREDIENTS

1/4 cup cocktail cranberry juice •2/3 cup firm silken tofu •1/2 cup frozen, unsweetened raspberries •1/2 cup frozen, unsweetened blueberries •1 teaspoon of vanilla extract

DIRECTIONS

- Pour the juice into a blender.
- Combine the remaining ingredients.
- Blend until completely smooth.
- Serve right away and enjoy!

Spicy Pina Colada Smoothie

Nutrition Facts (Per Serving) Calories 189 cal Fat 5g Sodium 5mg Carbs 32gProtein 13.4g Potassium 349 mg Phosphorus 121g

Prep time: 5 minutes Total time: 5 minutes Serving size 2 servings

INGREDIENTS

1 cup fresh or canned pineapple •1 cup (8 ounce) firm tofu •1/2 cup unsweetened pineapple juice •1 teaspoon of Stevia or other sweetness •1 tsp. red pepper flakes

DIRECTIONS

- In a blender, combine all of the ingredients.
- Serve right away and enjoy

Peach Raspberry Smoothie

Nutrition Facts (Per Serving) Calories 129 cal Fat 3.2g Sodium 53 mg Carbs 23g Protein 6.3g Potassium 261 mg Phosphorus 72g

Prep time: 5 minutes Total time: 5 minutes Serving 3 servings Serving size: 1 cup smoothie

INGREDIENTS

1 cup of raspberries, frozen •1 medium peach, pit taken out, and slices •1/2 cup of tofu •1 tablespoon honey (or add stevia or as a sweetener) •1 cup almond milk without additives

DIRECTIONS

- Blend all ingredients together in a blender until completely smooth.
- Serve and have pleasure!

POULTRY

Summer Pot Pie

Lime Grilled Turkey

Persian Chicken

Turkey Meatballs with Hot Sauce

Chicken Salad with Cranberries and Tarragon

Herb and Ricotta Stuffed Chicken

Oven Roasted Chicken and Warm Mushroom Salad with Watercress

Jerk Chicken Wings

Barbecue Chicken Salad

Chicken in Mushroom Sauce

Summer Pot Pie

Nutrition Facts (Per Serving) Calories 358 cal Fat 21g Sodium 188 mg Carbs 22g Protein 21g Potassium 432 mg Phosphorus 187g

Prep time: 15 minutes Total time: 45 minutes Serving size 1 cup 6 servings

INGREDIENTS

1 finely chopped onion •2 peeled and sliced carrots •1 cup (250 mL) green beans, chopped into 1/2-inch (1-cm) pieces, or 1 cup frozen green peas •Canola oil (60 mL) 1/4 cup •2 skinless, boneless chicken breast halves, cubed •2 garlic cloves, finely chopped •1/4 cup unbleached all-purpose flour (60 mL) •2 cups chicken broth (low sodium) •1 cup cauliflower, chopped into tiny florets •1/4 cup chopped parsley (60 mL) •4 oz (115 g) thawed frozen phyllo dough, cut into 1/4-inch (1/2-cm) thick slices •2 tbsp. (30 mL) canola oil

DIRECTIONS

- Season with pepper to taste
- Set the center rack in the oven and preheat it to 350°F.
- Soft onion, carrots, and green beans or peas in the oil for 8 minutes over medium heat in a pot.
- Cook until the chicken is lightly browned.
- With pepper or other spices, season to taste.
- Turn the heat down to medium.
- Cook the garlic for one minute after adding it.
- Toss in the flour and mix to blend.
- Bring the chicken stock to a boil while continually stirring it.
- On low heat, simmer for two to three minutes.
- Stir in the cauliflower and parsley until fully combined.
- Season with salt and pepper to taste. Fill a 15-cm (6-inch) square baking dish halfway with the batter.

- Place aside.
- Spread the phyllo dough strips on a baking sheet and sprinkle with the oil.
- Gently toss. Scatter over the vegetable mixture lightly, without pushing.
- Bake the pastry for about 30 minutes, or until golden brown.
- Enjoy

Lime Grilled Turkey

Nutrition Facts (Per Serving) Calories 245 cal Fat 15g Sodium 35mg Carbs 11.5g Protein 17.1g Potassium 200mg Phosphorus 131g

Prep time: 15 minutes Total time: 45 minutes Serving size 1/2 turkey slice breasts 4 servings

INGREDIENTS

125 mL (1/2 cup) of lime juice •60 ml or 1/4 cup of vegetable oil •2 tablespoons (30 mL) liquid honey •1 teaspoon (5 mL) dried thyme leaves •1 tsp (5 mL) dried rosemary •turkey breast, skinless and boneless, 2 3 lbs (300 g)

DIRECTIONS

- Combine the first five ingredients to make the marinade.
- Save two tablespoons (30 mL) of the marinade for basting.
- To create thinner pieces, slice the turkey breast in half lengthwise (much like you would a hamburger bun).
- Include the turkey in the marinade and refrigerate for one to two hours.
- Heat a barbecue or the broiler on high (500°F).
- To cook a turkey completely, broil or grill it for 4 minutes on each side.
- To baste the turkey while it cooks, use the marinade that was put aside in step 2.
- Throw away any extra marinade.
- Enjoy

Persian Chicken

Nutrition Facts (Per Serving) Calories 361 cal Fat 15g Sodium 86 mg Carbs 3g Protein 22g Potassium 253 mg Phosphorus 159g

Prep time: 15 minutes Total time: 1 hour 10 minutes Serving 10 Serving size 1 chicken thigh

INGREDIENTS

1 big, chopped onion •1/2 cup lemon juice, fresh •2 tablespoons of dried oregano •2 teaspoons of sweet paprika •2 teaspoons of minced garlic •1 cup of olive oil •10 skinless, boneless thighs of chicken

DIRECTIONS

- Puree the onion, lemon juice, oregano, paprika, and garlic in a food processor or blender.
- Add the oil gradually while the motor is running. Put the marinade and the chicken in a large, resealable plastic bag.
- Seal the bag securely after squeezing out the air.
- After turning the bag to disperse the marinad, chill for an hour.
- Take the chicken out of the marinade and discard any leftover marinade.
- For about 10 minutes, grill the chicken over direct, medium heat, flipping once.
- Make sure that the inside is completely pink-free and 165°F throughout.
- Enjoy with a green salad and some rice!

Turkey Meatballs with Hot Sauce

Nutrition Facts (Per Serving) Calories 68.4cal Fat 3.1g Sodium 58mg Carbs 3.7g Protein 5.7g Potassium 88 mg Phosphorus 100g

Prep time: 15 minutes Total time: 20 minutes Serving 15 Serving size 3 meatballs

INGREDIENTS

One pound of ground turkey •1 white egg •1/2 cup rich coffee (non-dairy creamer) •1/4 cup bell pepper, minced •1/4 cup onion, minced •1/2 cup unsalted bread crumbs •2 teaspoons Italian seasoning •1 teaspoon low-sodium soy sauce •1/2 cup apple jam •1/2 teaspoon cayenne pepper

DIRECTIONS

- Preheat the oven to 400°F.
- In a large mixing bowl, combine all ingredients except the jelly and cayenne pepper. Form into 45 meatballs.
- Bake the meatballs for about 20 minutes, or until cooked through.
- Microwave the jelly and cayenne pepper for 1 minute, or until liquefied.
- Place the meatballs in a serving dish and cover with jelly.
- Use toothpicks to serve.

Chicken Salad with Cranberries and Tarragon

Nutrition Facts (Per Serving) Calories 368cal Fat 9g Sodium 443 mg Carbs 42g Protein 26.5g Potassium 258 mg Phosphorus 233g

Prep time: 15 minutes Total time: 20 minutes Serving 4 Serving size 1 sandwich

INGREDIENTS

2-cups worth of cooked and chopped chicken meat •1/4 cup coarsely chopped dried cranberries •1 tablespoon minced shallots •1 teaspoon lemon juice •Mayonnaise, 1/4 cup •1 tsp freshly minced tarragon •1/2 teaspoon black pepper •8 slices of white bread

DIRECTIONS

- All the ingredients , except the bread, should be mixed in a bowl.
- Make four sandwiches by gently pushing together bread and chicken salad.
- Serve and take pleasure in

Herb and Ricotta Stuffed Chicken

Nutrition Facts (Per Serving) Calories 277cal Fat 13g Sodium 181.5mg Carbs 5g Protein 32g Potassium 353 mg Phosphorus 387g

Prep time: 15 minutes Total time: 20 minutes Serving 4 Serving size 1/2 chicken breast

INGREDIENTS

1 sautéed garlic clove •Extra virgin olive oil, 1 tablespoon •Ricotta, 1. 5 cups •1 egg •1/4 cup of chopped herbs •1/4 teaspoon black pepper •2 big (6 ounce) boneless, skinless chicken breasts

DIRECTIONS

- In olive oil, sauté the garlic.
- Mix the ricotta, eggs, herbs, and garlic.
- Make a slit in the chicken breast's fattest side.
- Put the mixture inside the chicken breast.
- Warm up the skillet's olive oil.
- Cook chicken in a pan, then place in a 350°F oven.
- Bake for around 20 to 30 minutes.
- Serve

Oven Roasted Chicken and Warm Mushroom Salad with Watercress

Nutrition Facts (Per Serving) Calories 340 cal Fat 13g Sodium 77mg Carbs 6g Protein 31g Potassium 420 mg Phosphorus 251g

Prep time: 15 minutes Total time: 20 minutes Serving 2 Serving size 1/2 of recipe

INGREDIENTS

2 breasts of chicken •Black peppercorns •4 tablespoons of olive oil •2 tablespoons of balsamic vinegar •1/2 teaspoon of thyme •1 cup of various wild mushrooms •1/2 cup of shallots •4 cups of watercress- and other mixed greens

DIRECTIONS

- Thyme and black pepper are used to season chicken.
- Add a drizzle of olive oil.
- Bake at 350°F until the center is no longer pink.
- In olive oil, sauté shallots and mushrooms. Thyme is used as a seasoning, followed by balsamic vinegar.
- Over a bed of greens, serve heated mushrooms and sliced chicken.

Jerk Chicken Wings

Nutrition Facts (Per Serving) Calories 382.4cal Fat 29.5g Sodium 84 mg Carbs 0.4g Protein 27.4g Potassium 194.6mg Phosphorus 155g

Prep time: 15 minutes Total time: 20 minutes Serving 6 Serving size 3 wings

Making this meal for a party is an excellent idea because everyone loves chicken wings.

INGREDIENTS

18 wings of chicken •1 teaspoon dried thyme •1 teaspoon all-spicy •1/2 tsp. cinnamon •Cayenne pepper, 1/3 tsp •Vegetable oil, 1/4 cup

DIRECTIONS

- Heat the oven to 450°F.
- To produce the **JERK** sauce, combine vegetable oil and dried spices.
- Sauce-baste chicken wings.
- For around 30-35 minutes, bake.
- Serve and enjoy !

Barbecue Chicken Salad

Nutrition Facts (Per Serving) Calories 171 cal Fat 5g Sodium 132 mg Carbs 5g Protein 25g Potassium 444 mg Phosphorus 203g

Prep time: 15 minutes Total time: 20 minutes Serving 8 Serving size ½ chicken breast + ½ cup veggies

INGREDIENTS

4 chicken breasts, skinless and without bones •5 mL (1 tsp) of soy sauce •Extra virgin olive oil, 2 tablespoons (30 mL). •2 tablespoons (30 mL) fresh cilantro •1 tablespoon (15 mL) minced ginger •2 garlic cloves •Red chili pepper flakes in the amount of half a teaspoon (2. 5 mL) •2 big yellow pepper •45 mL or 3 tbsp of rice vinegar •5 1/2 cups (1. 375 L) assorted salad greens

DIRECTIONS

- Fresh cilantro, minced. Mix the soy sauce, ginger, garlic, cilantro, and pepper flakes in a large bowl with the other half of the oil.
- Add the chicken breasts and stir to evenly coat.
- For at least 30 minutes or up to a day, cover and chill.
- Peppers should be quartered in the interim. A medium-high heat setting should be used for the grill.
- Grill peppers for around 15 minutes, or until they barely begin to turn black.
- Transfer to a plate. Grill chicken breasts for 10–15 minutes on each side, or until a thermometer inserted into the breast registers 165°F (74°C), over an oiled grill set to medium-high heat.

- Slice the chicken and heated grilled peppers into 1/2-inch broad strips. Toss the greens, remaining oil, and vinegar with the peppers and chicken in a large salad bowl.

Chicken in Mushroom Sauce

Nutrition Facts (Per Serving) Calories 161 cal Fat 4g Sodium 99 mg Carbs 5g Protein 25.6g Potassium 289 mg Phosphorus 205g

Prep time: 15 minutes Total time: 20 minutes Serving 8 Serving size 1/2 chicken breast and 1/8th of mushroom sauce

INGREDIENTS

1/4 cup all-purpose flour •2 tablespoons mild sour cream •1 tbsp Dijon Mustard •1 cup chicken broth (choose a brand with no salt added) •(Not "seasoned") 4 chicken breasts •1/4 teaspoon dried thyme •1 tbsp unsaturated margarine •1 1/2 cups quartered mushrooms •3 green onions, chopped •To taste, add freshly ground pepper and minced fresh parsley.

DIRECTIONS

- Combine 2 teaspoons of flour, 2 tablespoons of chicken stock, sour cream, and mustard. Place aside.
- Thyme and pepper should be added to the chicken before dredging in flour.
- Margarine should be melted in a large non-stick pan over low heat.
- Cook the chicken for 5 minutes on each side, or until the interior is no longer pink.
- Keep the chicken warm after removing it.
- Add the mushrooms to the pan and stir-fry for three minutes.
- Turn the heat up to high, add the last of the chicken stock, and simmer for three minutes.
- Add green onions after whisking in the sour cream mixture. 3 minutes

should be spent stirring, or until the mixture thickens.

- Pour over the chicken, add pepper and parsley on top, and then serve

Every bite you take can make a difference in your health - choose wisely with a renal diet

Enjoy a refreshing, delicious kidney-friendly beverage

BEVERAGES

Apple Cider Smash

Cranberry Mint Mocktail

Pineapple Punch

Fresh Lemonade with Mint

Lime and Mint Soda

Apple Cider Smash

Nutrition Facts (Per Serving) Calories 100.9cal Fat 0.1g Sodium   12.8mg Carbs 18.6g Protein 0.1g Potassium 23.8mg Phosphorus 2.7g

Prep time: 5 minutes Total time: 5 minutes Serving 2 servings Serving size: ½ the recipe

INGREDIENTS

1 cup of warm apple cider •1 ounce of spiced rum •1 teaspoon of cinnamon •2 apple slices

DIRECTIONS

- Fill two glasses with apple cider and spiced rum.
- Garnish with apple slices and cinnamon.

You may drink this beverage hot or chilled.

Cranberry Mint Mocktail

Nutrition Facts (Per Serving) Calories 7.9cal Fat 0.1g Sodium 23.4mg Carbs 18.6g Protein 0.3g Potassium 40 mg Phosphorus 5.5g

Prep time: 5 minutes Total time: 5 minutes Serving 2 servings Serving size: ½ the recipe

INGREDIENTS

2 tablespoons of mint, split •2 TBSP of split fresh cranberries •1 cup diet cranberry drink (split) •1/2 cup sparkling water, split •4 cubes of ice

DIRECTIONS

- Two glasses should be filled with mint and cranberries.
- Each glass should contain water and cranberry juice.
- To enjoy, add ice.

Pineapple Punch

Nutrition Facts (Per Serving) Calories 20.3cal Fat 0.1g Sodium 2.6mg Carbs 5.3g Protein 0.2g Potassium 4.6mg Phosphorus 60.7g

Prep time: 5 minutes Total time: 5 minutes Serving 2 servings Serving size: ½ the recipe

INGREDIENTS

4 tablespoons of pineapple juice •2 tablespoons of lime juice •1 cup of sparkling water •4 cubes of ice

DIRECTIONS

- Mix pineapple juice, lime juice, and water in a pitcher.
- Gently blend by stirring.
- Punch should be poured over ice-cubed serving glasses.
- Serve with fruit for an optional garnish, such as lime, berries, or mint.

Fresh Lemonade with Mint

Nutrition Facts (Per Serving) Calories 81 cal Carbs 21.1g Potassium 16mg Phosphorus 1g

Prep time: 5 minutes Total time: 5 minutes Serving 5 servings Serving size: 3/4 cup (175 ml)

INGREDIENTS

3 fresh medium lemons •1/2 cup (125 ml) white sugar •6 fresh mint leaves •Half a cup (125 ml) of boiling water •3 cups (750 ml of cold water)

DIRECTIONS

- Mix hot water and sugar in a 5-cup (1. 25-liter) pitcher.
- Stir the sugar until it dissolves.
- Add two lemons' juice and some mint leaves.
- Add the remaining lemon to the pitcher after slicing it thinly.
- Stir in some ice-cold water.
- Before serving, chill.

For optimal flavor, let it chill overnight.

Ideas for serving: Include a pic of fresh mint.

Lime and Mint Soda

Nutrition Facts (Per Serving) Calories 31.3cal Fat 0.6g Sodium 6.9mg Protein 0.2g Carbs 8.7g Potassium 95.7mg Phosphorus 13.6g

Prep time: 5 minutes Total time: 5 minutes Serving 2 servings Serving size: ½ the recipe

INGREDIENTS

4 tablespoons of mint leaves •1 lime, cut into quarters •2 tablespoons of lime cordial •1 cup of sparkling water •4 cubes of ice

DIRECTIONS

- In a bowl or pestle, combine the lime and mint.
- Carefully pound limes with the end of a pestle or spoon until juice is extracted.
- Divide the lime and mint into the two mugs.
- In each cup, combine the mint mixture with the cordial and ice. Pour sparkling water over top.
- Serve and have pleasure!

FISH & SEAFOODS

Fish Tacos

Tuna Spread

Spaghetti with Shrimp

Chili Aioli Shrimp Dip

Tortilla Pizza with Roasted Red Pepper Pesto, Shrimp and Basil

Fish Tacos

Nutrition Facts (Per Serving) Calories 227.2cal Fat 6.8g Sodium 99.3mg Carbs 12.9 g Protein 27.6g Potassium 324.47mg Phosphorus 235.01 mg

Prep time: 5 minutes Total time: 5 minutes Servings per recipe: 8

INGREDIENTS

Eight corn tortillas •2 pounds of cod fish •1 tablespoon of Chipotle powder •3 tablespoons of vegetable oil •3 tablespoons of all-purpose flour •Lettuce and lime wedges (for garnish)

DIRECTIONS

- Heat oil in a pan. Fish should be dredged in a basin with flour and chipotle sauce.
- Pan-fry the fish until it reaches a temperature of 145°F.
- Warm tortillas in the oven while wrapped in a tea towel.
- Serve the fish with lime juice squeezed over it.
- Serve alongside steamed veggies, green salad, or cole slaw.

Tuna Spread

Nutrition Facts (Per Serving) Calories 101 cal Fat 4.9g Sodium 37 mg Carbs 1.3g Protein 12.4g Potassium 91 mg Phosphorus 133 mg

Prep time: 5 minutes Total time: 5 minutes Servings per recipe: 4 Serving size: 1/4 cup

INGREDIENTS

1 can (170 g) of drained, no-salt-added tuna •2 tablespoons of light mayo •1 teaspoon lemon juice •1/2 tsp. mustard Dijon •Season with pepper to taste

DIRECTIONS

- Use a fork to stir all the ingredients together in a bowl.
- Use pepper to season.
- Serve with bread or crackers.

Advice: Opt for tuna that is packed in water rather than oil if you want to further minimize your calorie intake.

Spaghetti with Shrimp

Nutrition Facts (Per Serving) Calories 716cal Fat 55g Sodium 326mg Carbs 25g Protein 28g Potassium 340 mg Phosphorus 215mg

Prep time: 5 minutes Total time: 5 minutes Servings per recipe: 4 Serving size: 1/4 cup

INGREDIENTS

1/2 pound of spaghetti •1/3 cup extra virgin olive oil •1/3 cup of dry white wine •2 smashed garlic cloves •1/4 teaspoon crushed red chilies •1 chopped red pepper •1 pound raw shrimp •1/3 cup freshly toasted breadcrumbs •Freshly ground black pepper **(Optional)** Fresh parsley chopped

DIRECTIONS

- Pasta should be prepared in accordance with the directions on the package.
- Heat the oil in a large pan over medium-low heat, then add the garlic and crushed red chilies.
- Cook for one minute while stirring.
- Add the peppers and simmer for another 5 minutes without browning.
- After adding the shrimp, heat for an additional minute.
- Put the heat on medium-high and add the wine.
- Simmer the shrimp until they become opaque and begin to curl. Keep the spaghetti warm over low heat if it is not yet cooked.
- Pasta should be drained and placed in a large serving dish.

- Pasta should be covered after being topped with sauce and tossed with breadcrumbs.
- Serve with parsley and freshly ground pepper.

Chili Aioli Shrimp Dip

Nutrition Facts (Per Serving) Calories 95cal Fat 10.4g Sodium 74.8mg Carbs 0.16g Protein 0.02g Potassium 4.3mg Phosphorus 0.57mg

Prep time: 5 minutes Total time: 5 minutes Servings per recipe: 19 Serving size: 1 TBSP

INGREDIENTS

One cup of Hellmann's mayo •1 teaspoon of Thai chili sauce •1–2 tablespoons chopped parsley •1/2 clove of minced garlic •1 teaspoon lemon juice

DIRECTIONS

- Combine all of the ingredients.
- Use it as a spread on a tomato sandwich made with fresh white bread or as a dip for shrimp cocktail.

Tortilla Pizza with Roasted Red Pepper Pesto, Shrimp and Basil

Nutrition Facts (Per Serving) Calories 246 cal Fat 11g Sodium 314 mg Carbs 26g Protein 19g Potassium 305mg Phosphorus 238mg

Prep time: 5 minutes Total time: 10 minutes Servings per recipe: 2 Serving size: 1 tortilla pizza

INGREDIENTS

To make the pizza:

8 big shrimp, skinned, deveined, and tail removed (31/40 count) •1/4 cup thinly chopped vidalia onions •6 basil leaves, torn or coarsely chopped •1/2 cup grated mozzarella cheese •2 tortillas (flour)

To make the pesto:

1 red pepper, roasted •1 clove of garlic •1 tablespoon of lemon juice •1 tablespoon of extra virgin olive oil •1/8 teaspoon of black pepper, ground •1 teaspoon of parmesan cheese, grated

DIRECTIONS

- Preheat the oven to 425°F (conventional oven).
- Blend or process all the ingredients for the pesto in a food processor.
- On a cookie sheet, arrange the flour tortillas.
- Between the two tortillas, divide the roasted red pepper pesto and spread it out evenly.
- Include the basil and onions.
- Add some mozzarella cheese.
- Place prawns on top of the pizzas after cutting them in half lengthwise.
- Bake for about 10 minutes, or until the shrimp becomes pink and the tortillas crisp and turn golden brown.

Your plant-based renal diet is an opportunity to nourish your body and delight your taste buds

VEGAN-PLANT-BASED RECIPES

Cucumber Salad

Garlic Green Beans Salad

Tarragon Dressing with Salad

Warm Mushroom Salad with Watercress

Roasted Cabbage Wedges

Cucumber Salad

Nutrition Facts (Per Serving) Calories 51cal Fat 11g Sodium 5mg Carbs 11g Protein 1g Potassium 130 mg Phosphorus 29mg

Prep time: 5 minutes Total time: 10 minutes Servings per recipe: 10 Serving size: 1/10 of recipe

INGREDIENTS

3 English cucumbers, either striped or peeled •1 large red onion •1/2 cup of rice vinegar •1/2 cup of water •1/3 cup of sugar **For garnish**, use 2 tablespoons of toasted white sesame seeds.

DIRECTIONS

- In a bowl, thinly slice cucumber into rounds and finely dice onion.
- Pour over the cucumber and onion after combining the rice vinegar, water, and sugar.
- Cover and set aside for an hour to marinate.
- Put sesame seeds on the plate as a garnish.
- Serve and enjoy

Garlic Green Beans Salad

Nutrition Facts (Per Serving) Calories 59 cal Fat 4g Sodium 2mg Carbs 6g Protein 1g Potassium 107 mg Phosphorus 22mg

Prep time: 5 minutes Total time: 10 minutes Servings per recipe: 4 Serving size: 1/2 of recipe

INGREDIENTS

2 cups of green beans •2 chopped garlic cloves •1 tablespoon balsamic or red wine vinegar •1 tablespoon of sesame oil

DIRECTIONS

- In boiling water, clean the beans and cook them until done.
- Drain, then refresh with ice-cold water.
- Combine the garlic, vinegar, and oil with the beans.

Tarragon Dressing with Salad

Nutrition Facts (Per Serving) Calories 97cal Fat 9.7g Sodium 14mg Carbs 2.6g Protein 0.8g Potassium 159.2mg Phosphorus 20mg

Prep time: 5 minutes Total time: 10 minutes Servings per recipe: 8 Serving size: 1 cup

INGREDIENTS

1 tsp of The Dijon Mustard •2 tablespoons of lemon juice •2 tablespoons of white wine vinegar •1 teaspoon of minced shallot •1 tsp dried tarragon or 2 tbsp fresh tarragon •1/3 cup extra virgin olive oil •8 cups of mixed or lettuce greens

DIRECTIONS

- To prepare, mince the shallots.
- Add the mustard, tarragon, vinegar, and lemon juice.
- Stir in the olive oil.
- Sprinkle over the greens.
- Serve and take pleasure in!

Warm Mushroom Salad with Watercress

Nutrition Facts (Per Serving) Calories 159 cal Fat 14g Sodium 26mg Carbs 7g Protein 2.2g Potassium 329 mg Phosphorus 54 mg

Prep time: 5 minutes Total time: 10 minutes Servings per recipe: 4 Serving size: 1/4 of the salad (about 1 1/2 cups)

INGREDIENTS

4 tablespoons of olive oil •2 tablespoons of balsamic vinegar •1/2 teaspoon of thyme •1 cup of a variety of mushrooms •1/2 cup of shallots •4 cups of mixed greens, including watercress

DIRECTIONS

- In olive oil, sauté shallots and mushrooms.
- Season with thyme and, afterwards, add balsamic vinegar.
- Serve over a bed of greens and have pleasure while eating.

Roasted Cabbage Wedges

Nutrition Facts (Per Serving) Calories 32.3cal Fat 1.8g Sodium 10.5mg Carbs 4.0g Protein 0.74g Potassium 15 mg Phosphorus 98 mg

Prep time: 5 minutes Total time: 25 minutes Servings per recipe: 16 Serving size: 1 wedge slice

INGREDIENTS

1 green cabbage, sliced into 1-inch wedges •2 teaspoons of sugar •¼ teaspoon of freshly ground pepper, or to taste •1 tablespoon of balsamic vinegar •2 tablespoons of olive oil

DIRECTIONS

- Bake sheet and oven at 450 °F.

- In a small bowl, mix the sugar and the pepper.

- Try to keep the cure intact when you quarter the cabbage through the center and cut each quarter into 1-inch wedges; this will keep the wedges from coming apart. There will be roughly 16 wedges.

- Slices are brushed with oil, then salt and pepper are added.

- Roast the seasoned wedges for about 25 minutes, or until the cabbage is soft and the edges are gently browned.

- Sprinkle balsamic vinegar over the cabbage

CONCLUSION

As we culminate this culinary expedition through the "Complete Healthy Renal Diet Cookbook for Beginners, " it is with immense satisfaction and a profound sense of purpose that we bring this journey to a close. This book, meticulously designed with your well-being in mind, has aimed to be more than just a collection of recipes; it is your compass towards a path of kidney health and a lifelong celebration of delicious, nourishing meals.

Throughout these pages, we have explored a rich tapestry of recipes that not only tantalize your palate but also serve as a powerful tool for nurturing your kidneys. The journey towards improved kidney health can indeed be daunting, yet with the right guidance and a touch of culinary creativity, it transforms into a rewarding voyage filled with flavors, health, and vitality.

We embarked on this endeavor with a clear mission: to empower you, our esteemed readers, with the knowledge and resources to take command of your diet and, consequently, your overall health. Each recipe presented in this cookbook was carefully created to strike a harmonious balance between culinary delight and the stringent requirements of a renal diet, ensuring that every meal you prepare is a delicious contribution to your health.

But the purpose of this book extends beyond providing recipes. It serves as your steadfast companion and guide to navigate the nuanced world of renal nutrition.

A renal diet, we understand, present unique challenges, yet it is a path rich in opportunities for growth and resourcefulness. As you approach each meal with intention and mindfulness, you transform your dietary choices into a potent tool for promoting kidney health and overall well-being.

In your pursuit of kidney health, we also remind you that you are not alone. Whether you are taking your initial steps on this path or have been journeying along it for some time, your commitment to kidney health is indeed commendable. Do not hesitate to seek support and guidance from healthcare professionals, dietitians, and fellow travelers on this path. Their shared experiences and expertise are invaluable resources.

"The Complete Healthy Renal Diet Cookbook for Beginners" aspires to be not just a cookbook but a companion, a source of inspiration, and a guardian of your well-being. As you relish each dish, may it remind you of the incredible journey you have embarked on—a journey where health, joy, and flavor are intertwined.

May the recipes you've discovered within these pages fuel your health, uplift your spirits, and illuminate your life. Here's to your health, your happiness, and your culinary adventure ahead.

In parting, we express our heartfelt gratitude for choosing this book as your culinary and wellness companion. Your journey towards kidney health is a testament to your dedication to self-care, and we celebrate every step you take. Your health is a priceless treasure, and this cookbook embodies our pledge to aid you in preserving it.

Warmest regards,

Gwendolyn . J. Hall

Your kidneys are your best friends - treat them well and they'll treat you well

May I make a special inquiry?

Dear Sir or Madam,

On your path to kidney health, I hope "**The Complete Healthy Renal Diet Cookbook for Beginners**" has been a useful tool. I value your opinion very much, so if you could spare a moment to write a review, I would be very appreciative of your views and experiences.

In addition to assisting me in making future editions better, your review will serve as a helpful resource for anybody looking for a reliable source to promote renal health. Your candid criticism may truly change things.

Just go to the website (like Amazon) where you bought the book to leave a review. Your suggestions are highly valued.

I appreciate your help and wish you all the best as you pursue your goals.

Warmest regards,

Gwendolyn . J. Hall

Every bite you take can make a difference in your health - choose wisely with a renal diet

Additional Information

If you've found inspiration and valuable insights in "The Complete Healthy Renal Diet Cookbook for Beginners," you're in for a delightful journey through a world of wellness and culinary exploration with Gwendolyn J. Hall.
As a dedicated author, Gwendolyn has crafted a collection of books that cater to a diverse range of interests and needs.

Whether you're seeking further culinary delights, wellness guides, personal development, or even captivating narratives, Gwendolyn's literary repertoire offers something for everyone. Her commitment to empowering readers with the knowledge and tools to lead healthier, more enriching lives shines through in every word she writes.

To embark on your next literary adventure, we invite you to explore Gwendolyn J. Hall's Author Central Page. There, you'll find a curated selection of her works, each brimming with wisdom, inspiration, and the joy of exploration. With every turn of the page, you'll discover the transformative power of Gwendolyn's literary offerings.

Visit Gwendolyn's Author Central Page now to uncover a world of possibilities and embark on a journey towards a more vibrant and fulfilled life. Your next great read awaits!

Explore More of Gwendolyn J. Hall's Literary World

https://www.amazon.com/author/gwendolyn.j.hall **OR** Scan the QR Code below

Turning the page to Wellness : Your 14-Day Renal Diet Roadmap In Between these pages.

21 Days Renal Diet Meal Plan

I promised you a 14-day meal plan, and it's right here, ready to transform your eating habits and energize your life. Get started on your journey today!

Days	Breakfast	Lunch	Dinner	Snacks / Desserts
Day 1	Blueberry Muffins	Egg Fried Rice	Spaghetti and Asparagus Carbonara	Sesame Carrots
Day 2	Chocolate Banana Oatmeal	Crunchy Quinoa Salad	Mashed Carrots & Ginger	Caramel Apples
Day 3	Southwest Baked Egg Breakfast Cups	Brussels sprouts Chips	Sesame Tuna Salad	Cucumber Bites
Day 4	Apple Oatmeal	Creamy Coleslaw	Easy Brown Rice	Gorp
Day 5	Maple Granola	Mediterranean Green Beans	Fish Tacos with Avocado-Lime Crema	Chocolate Nut Bark
Day 6	Pineapple Smoothie	Hawaiian Turkey Sliders	Easy Brown Rice	Mini Pecan Pies

Day 7	Southwest Baked Egg Breakfast Cups	Margherita Pizza	Vinegary Coleslaw	Indoor S'more
Day 8	Summer Pot Pie	Pumpkin Strudel	Sautéed Collard Greens	Watermelon Fruit Pizza
Day 9	Cucumber Salad	Peanut Butter Oats Energy Balls	Cabbage - Onion - Sweet Pepper Medley	Roasted Garlic and Ricotta Crostini
Day 10	Fish Tacos	Tomato Phyllo Tart	Broccoli-Bacon Salad	Apple Cider Smash
Day 11	Garlic Green Beans Salad	Crispy Cauliflower Phyllo Cups Recipe	Strawberry Fruit Salad	Pineapple Punch
Day 12	Tuna Spread	Cucumber & Tomato Salad with Preserved Lemon	Chicken & Fruit Salad	Fruity Smoothie
Day 13	Persian Chicken	Rustic Mushroom Tart	Cool and Crispy Cucumber	Mixed Berry Protein Smoothie
Day 14	Roasted Pumpkin Seeds	Chili Cornbread Casserole	Broccoli-Bacon Salad	Homemade Trail Mix

Stay curious, keep exploring new recipes, and, most importantly, take charge of your well-being.